Love of Learning

Supporting Intrinsic Motivation in Montessori Students

Michael and D'Neil Duffy

Illustrated By
Laini Szostkowski

BOOKS·ART

A division of Montessori Services
www.MontessoriServices.com

Book Design By Holly Weetman

Parent Child Press
A Division of Montessori Services
11 West 9th Street
Santa Rosa, CA 95401

Visit our website at www.MontessoriServices.com

First Edition: March 2012

This book is dedicated to our grandchildren—

Ben, Rebecca, Mya and Ava.

Other Books available at Parent Child Press

Children of the Universe:
Cosmic Education in the Montessori Classroom

Math Works: Montessori Math and the Developing Brain

The Deep Well of Time:
The Transformative Power of Storytelling in the Classroom

Nurturing the Spirit in Non-Sectarian Classrooms

Montessori for a Better World

A Parents' Guide to the Montessori Classroom

Montessori Insights for Parents of Young Children

The Peace Rose

Our Peaceful Classroom

Living, Creating, Sharing — A Montessori Life

Color Clues for Vowel Sounds

Andy and His Daddy

I Wonder What's Out There:
A Vision of the Universe for Primary Classes

Thoughtful Living Series

Cosmic Wonder Series

Child-Size Masterpieces, a series of eight books of art postcards

www.MontessoriServices.com

Love of Learning

Supporting Intrinsic Motivation
in Montessori Students

Table of Contents

Introduction

How do we motivate Montessori students to love learning the way Maria Montessori said they would? She painted a picture of normalized students willingly engaged in concentrated work and excited to discover new knowledge. The reality of the modern Montessori elementary classroom does not always reflect this ideal. Why?

As we work with Montessori teachers in teacher training courses, in classroom visits, and in school consultations, one of the biggest problems we encounter is a struggle to operate classrooms effectively in a Montessori manner. We have all worked hard to master the Montessori method of education and are disillusioned when our students do not respond the way we anticipated from our training.

Some new Montessori teachers may be very effective in giving lessons but less so in keeping students on task and displaying appropriate behavior. They may not yet have completely internalized the overarching philosophical principles that are the foundation for Montessori classroom practice.

Others, perhaps very experienced teachers, may have lost sight of those guiding principles over the years, gradually abandoning genuine Montessori practice in a slow erosion of what seemed like small compromises along the way. The result is a classroom that has come to resemble traditional education in more ways than are desirable.

Even teachers who have stayed true to Montessori principles and classroom practice struggle with a few stray students who don't get engaged in their work very easily and who need constant re-direction. They may have exhausted their ideas of how to stimulate these unmotivated students and to involve them in independent learning.

Those kinds of struggles that we all face are the rationale for this book, and our suggestions are meant to spark a dialogue with you as our colleagues. The book is geared primarily to assist Montessori elementary teachers to become more effective guides for their students and to cope with the frustrations all teachers feel at times.

While we don't claim to have all the answers to these troubling issues, we hope our experience in working with hundreds of Montessori schools and teachers over the past few decades and our study of modern experts will allow us to share some useful guidance with teachers—whether they are brand new to the classroom or whether they are trying to rekindle their initial enthusiasm years down the road.

Part 1 is our attempt to synthesize Maria Montessori's scattered ideas about motivation into a coherent theory. It takes the reader through a systematic review of the fundamental principles on which classroom practice is based. Each chapter also includes a discussion of non-Montessori educational literature that supports the Montessori theory and that offers additional insights for us to consider.

In Part 2, we offer suggestions for strategies to help motivate our students, from Montessori's insights, from our own experience and from modern authors. This part draws heavily on Alfie Kohn and Daniel Pink, among others, who have explored the research on intrinsic motivation and have many helpful suggestions to offer.

This book is a combination of our own knowledge and experience and that of our colleagues at the Montessori Elementary Teacher Training Collaborative (METTC), many of whom we have worked with for over a quarter century, including decades at the Center for Montessori Teacher Education/New York before METTC assumed responsibility for the elementary training from CMTE/NY in 2013.

No teacher is perfect, no educational theory is completely successful, and no child is quite like any other child. In particular, there may be some children who have underlying emotional problems or learning difficulties that need to be identified and remediated before any of these suggestions will produce significant results.

However, if our work helps Montessori elementary teachers inspire at least some of their seemingly unmotivated students to acquire a genuine love of learning, we will be satisfied with our efforts.

Part 1
Montessori and Motivation

Philosophical Principles
and Resulting Theory

Chapter 1

Self-Discipline:
A Radical Paradigm for Students

Maria Montessori never wrote a book specifically about motivation. Her ideas are spread throughout many of her books, but there is a coherent theory that emerges from a careful reading of all those sources.

Montessori, somewhat ahead of her time, came to believe that motivation for learning should come from inside children rather than being imposed from outside by an adult. In other words, she favored the intrinsic motivation model that has become more in vogue since the 1960s over the extrinsic motivation paradigm that dominated education for centuries.

Her theory is rooted in her ideas about what we traditionally refer to as "discipline" and "classroom management." These are pre-requisites for motivation in a classroom. Without a disciplined classroom atmosphere, students can't really focus in any sustained way that we would describe as motivated.

However, Montessori's approach to these two subjects is quite different than what we might find in traditional settings. Both of the traditional terms imply too much control for Montessori. What she was really talking about was the development of the child's *self-discipline*, with the teacher assuming the important role of *community leadership*.

We will elaborate on these two themes in the first two chapters as the essential conditions required for the emergence of *autonomous learning* or *auto-education* in Montessori philosophy, the subject of Chapter 3. Auto-education is the radically different approach to education that Montessori embraces as the heart of her method. This, in turn, is the foundation for Montessori's belief in *intrinsic motivation,* the subject of Chapter 4. Auto-education demands intrinsic motivation as an essential component and, at the same time, provides the foundation for motivation the way Montessori envisioned it.

That's a quick summary of Part 1. Let's take a look at the details.

Self-Discipline in Montessori Philosophy

"A room in which all the children move about usefully, intelligently, and voluntarily, without committing any rough or rude act, would seem to be a classroom very well disciplined indeed."[1]

How does our classroom come to look like the calm, orderly place described above? Certainly not on the first day of the school year —it takes time for students to get into the flow of Montessori. There is a hum of busy activity in a Montessori classroom that depends on what she called the "normalization" of the child.

"Only 'normalized' children, aided by their environment, show in their subsequent development those wonderful powers that we describe: spontaneous discipline, continuous and happy work, social sentiments of help and sympathy for others," she wrote.[2]

Montessori believed that children's "normal" state is to be absorbed in the task of building themselves into adults—to be motivated to work and to learn—and that misbehavior represents a "deviation" that must be corrected by immersion in meaningful activity.

"Normalization comes about through 'concentration' on a piece of work. For this we must provide 'motives for activity' so well adapted to the child's interest that they provoke his deep attention...*The essential thing is for the task to arouse such an interest that it engages the child's whole personality.*"[3]

---

[1]Montessori, Maria, *The Montessori Method* (New York: Schocken Books, 1964), 93.
[2]Montessori, Maria, *The Absorbent Mind* (New York: Dell Publishing, 1984), 206.
[3]Montessori, *Absorbent,* 206.

Normalization, and the resulting motivation that it supports, does not occur magically. It takes time and effort to bring about this level of internal development on the part of the children.

Although Montessori used the term primarily for individuals, we often refer to a classroom as normalized once the majority of children have been individually normalized. This is particularly appropriate for the elementary level, where the social element becomes so important.

Typically, at the beginning of the school year in a class filled with new children and others returning from a long vacation, the class is far from normalized. Then, weeks or sometimes even months into the school year, there is a transformation of the atmosphere of the class into the quiet, busy hum of activity we call normalized.

This does not happen because we, the teachers, have intimidated the students into submission. Over time, the students begin to spend more time engaged with the materials in the different subject areas. As they become involved in academic work, a calmer atmosphere emerges, a "settling down to business" takes hold.

The goal for us is not to discipline children by forcing them to be quiet, immobile and passive; Montessori insisted that the goal is to promote student activity.[4] Children should not act out of fear of being punished by a stronger, larger person, or for the sake of reward from the adult. Their discipline is meant to come from inside themselves in what can only be called *self-discipline.* A child is "disciplined when he is master of himself and can therefore regulate his own behavior."[5]

Montessori devotes two chapters to the theme of discipline in *The Montessori Method* and she addresses the issue in other writings as well. In *The Absorbent Mind*, for example, she relates the story of an "old-fashioned" visitor to the school approaching a young child and asking him, "So this is the school where you do as you like?"

"No ma'am," said the child. "It is not that we do as we like, but we like what we do."[6]

---

[4]Montessori, *Method,* 93.
[5]Ibid, 86.
[6]Montessori, *Absorbent,* 249.

That distinction, grasped instinctively by this young child, is at the heart of the way Montessori understands discipline and motivation. For her, discipline is not something imposed on children by an adult— it is something that springs from inside children in response to their experience of successfully pursuing their self-development through meaningful activity.

Her counter-intuitive approach to discipline is "based on liberty," something she said should be particularly appealing to an American audience of readers.[7] It is not by repressing the freedom of the children that self-discipline is attained; it is precisely by enlarging their scope of liberty that children are free to actively engage in work that allows them to achieve that self-discipline, something quite different from society's usual ideas about discipline.

"Such discipline could never be obtained by commands, by sermonizing, in short, through any of the disciplinary devices universally known...it certainly does not depend upon the teacher but upon a sort of miracle, occurring in the inner life of the child," she wrote.[8]

What drives this movement toward self-discipline is work that promotes the internal development of the child. Everything children do to help them grow internally toward the adult persons they choose to become produces a sense of intense joy and satisfaction within them.

"The first dawning of real discipline comes through work. At a given moment it happens that a child becomes keenly interested in a piece of work, showing it by the expression of his face, by his intense attention, by his perseverance in the same exercise. That child has set foot upon the road leading to discipline."[9]

Montessori believed that it was through this engagement with work that children fulfilled their natural, internal drive to self-development, leading in turn to self-discipline. "His own self-development is his true and almost his only pleasure," she said.[10]

She interprets some forms of a child's misbehavior as righteous rebellion against being "forced away from his mission in life." For

---

[7]Montessori, *Method,* 346.
[8]Ibid, 349.
[9]Ibid, 350.
[10]Ibid, 356.

example, he may be forbidden to speak with his peers when they are central to his stage of development, or he may be forced to sit immobile when everything in him calls for movement. "He shows himself to be a rebel, a revolutionist, an iconoclast, against those who do not understand him and who, fancying that they are helping him, are really pushing him backward in the highway of life."[11]

She speaks out forcefully against adult interventions that limit the child's independence, that suffocate independent activity, that sap his capacity to act on his own and hinder the development of his natural forces.

Montessori does advocate "obedience," although she uses the term in a different way than we usually think of it. For her, obedience does not signify subservience of the child to the will of the adult, but rather the development of the will of the child for self-discipline. Modern authors use terms like executive function and impulse control, but the old-fashioned terminology of *will* is essentially what is involved.

From a positive point of view, obedience involves the child using his will to complete coordinated actions towards a specific end and achieving something he has chosen to do; obedience also has an inhibitive role, using will power to avoid acting impulsively and patiently repeating an activity before abandoning it.[12]

This development of the will of the child comes about in stages, partly because of the need to exercise his will and partly because the child at a young age lacks the physical control that would allow him to accomplish what he wishes to do. Montessori speaks of a first stage in the development of the will when a child simply cannot do a specified activity, a second stage when he can do it sometimes, and a third stage when he can do it always.[13]

What moves the child from one stage to another is partly a matter of maturation, of strengthening his will and his ability to carry out the commands of his own will. It is also partly a growing recognition of the child that liberty is not without limits, that obedience is a necessary part of living in society or in a community.

---

[11] Montessori, *Method*, 359.
[12] Ibid, 364.
[13] Ibid, 367.

When children achieve a level of will power for purposeful activity and recognize the limits on their freedom in a community, they are able to express themselves with self-discipline. This is the equivalent to learning to act in a moral or ethical manner, something Montessori believed could not be achieved in any meaningful way until children reached their elementary years.

Robert Coles, a modern expert on the moral development of children, validates Montessori's vision of the "moral" child emerging in the elementary years. This is the age when children develop a conscience, an internal compass or code of conduct that allows them to make good moral or ethical choices.[14]

So it is a mistake to think that this is a process that is completed when a child turns six or seven. Throughout the elementary years, children continue to fine-tune their moral sense, to experiment with the limits imposed on their freedom by their community of peers. Most of them have not reached the third stage of obedience of which Montessori spoke or the highest level of moral decision-making that writers like Coles describe. They are simply on the way.

That means their behavior can at times continue to be inappropriate for the classroom, and not every moment is going to be one that reflects a normalized child. The more they become engaged in their work, however, the more they and the classroom begin to look like that described by Montessori.

She speaks with pride about the atmosphere in these classrooms, and she notes that visitors to well-run Montessori classrooms are instantly struck by the fact that the children are generally better behaved than students in traditional classrooms.

We saw a dramatic illustration of this in our work with Montessori teachers from public schools in Puerto Rico over the past five years. As we visited their schools, we were constantly impressed by the stark contrast between the loud, chaotic behavior displayed by students in the traditional classrooms and the calm, almost Zen-like atmosphere in the Montessori classrooms.

The model of these individual classrooms within a larger, public school community of mostly poor, inner city children was a striking

---

[14] Coles, Robert, *The Moral Intelligence of Children* (New York: Random House, 1997), 98 ff.

enough contrast to entice other teachers in these schools to seek Montessori training themselves, and the work of transformation continues at a dozen different "sister" schools.

So, with a Montessori approach, it is clearly possible to have well functioning classrooms if the students are self-disciplined.

The Non-Montessori Literature on Positive Discipline

Do experts outside the Montessori community agree that this sort of self-discipline is possible for young school children? Are there further strategies that modern authors offer on the subject that are consistent with the Montessori philosophy and from which we can learn?

There is an entire body of literature that promotes the idea of building a child's sense of responsibility as the primary means of discipline. These approaches attempt to gradually eliminate the authoritarian role of the adult as the preferred form of discipline. As physical punishment such as spankings lost favor in the 1960s and subsequent decades, numerous experts began promoting a more *positive discipline* for both parents and teachers.

One of the earliest and most influential proponents of this approach was Dr. Rudolf Dreikurs, a child psychiatrist. In his book, *Children: The Challenge*, Dreikurs tried to teach parents how to defuse confrontations with their children, encouraging them to understand the goals of misbehavior and to allow natural and logical consequences to occur. [15]

Dreikurs, who put into practice the theories of the famous psychologist Alfred Adler (a contemporary of Maria Montessori), noted that to achieve discipline within a child, we must first understand the motivation for his behavior. From a positive point of view, he maintains that a child's "strongest motivation is the desire to belong...Everything he does is aimed at finding his place."[16]

When a child acts in a negative or inappropriate way, Dreikurs argues, it is often because of a mistaken or misguided way of achieving

---

[15]Dreikurs, Rudolf, *Children: The Challenge* (New York: Hawthorn Books, 1964). He also wrote *The Challenge of Parenthood, Discipline without Tears,* and *Logical Consequences.*
[16]Ibid, 14.

that desire to belong: a desire for undue attention, a struggle for power, a search for retaliation or revenge, or a demonstration of complete inadequacy. Only by understanding the child's hidden motives can we effectively address his needs and produce a positive outcome.[17] Like Montessori, he argues that it is not the adult's role to put effort into "molding the child's character," but rather to allow children to "shape and mold themselves."[18]

A major tenet of Dreikurs is that parents—and teachers—need to abandon their reliance on punishments and rewards in favor of a system of natural and logical consequences.[19] The punishment/reward approach stems from a desire to manipulate children into compliance with adult wishes; the latter shifts the emphasis to the consequences of choices the child himself makes, leading over time to the kind of responsible decision making and self-discipline Montessori advocated.

Some consequences are natural outcomes of choices. For example, if a child forgets his lunch, he will be hungry at school; or if he oversleeps, he will be late for school and perhaps miss the chance to sit next to his best friend. There is no need for an adult to intervene or invoke those outcomes for them to occur.

As for logical consequences, Dreikurs uses the example of a child resisting her parent's insistence that she eat dinner. The logical consequence, after the parents remove the food from the table, is that the child goes to bed hungry.

Dreikurs maintains that natural consequences always achieve their effect, as long as parents don't rescue their children. Logical consequences, which involve intervention on the part of the adult, can easily be turned into a punishment if they are used as a threat or post-facto imposition of pain and misery.

The purpose of using consequences is to move children toward self-discipline. Dreikurs maintains this requires a "reorientation on the part of our thinking. We must realize that we no longer live in an autocratic society that can 'control' children but in a democratic society that needs

---

[17]Dreikurs, *Children: The Challenge,* 58-64.
[18]Ibid, 32.
[19]Ibid, 76-85.

to 'guide' them. We can no longer impose our will on children. We must now 'stimulate' proper behavior."[20]

Another useful resource is *The Discipline Book* by William and Martha Sears, from their perspectives as parents and as a pediatrician and a registered nurse. The premise on which they base their whole book is the belief that "discipline depends on *building the right relationship with a child.*"[21]

This fits well with Montessori philosophy and with our own observations of successful Montessori teachers. The difference between teachers who succeed and those who fail is often rooted in whether the teacher has a healthy relationship with her students, winning their respect because she relates to them with understanding, wins their trust, and makes them feel safe and supported.

Like others whom we cite here, they say that the goal of discipline is "helping your child develop *inner controls* that last a lifetime."[22] In fact, they describe discipline in an eloquent way that deserves to be quoted in full:

"Disciplining children means equipping them with the tools to succeed in life. One of the most important tools is the ability to make right choices. To do so, a child needs to develop social sensitivity, the ability to consider how his actions will affect other people. Call it instilling values, call it developing a conscience, but whatever you call it, one of your jobs as a disciplinarian is to help your child develop an internal guidance system that steers him in the right direction when you're not there to help him make the best choice. This is discipline for life."[23]

While the authors are speaking mainly to parents, their words are equally appropriate for teachers. Their summary of the purpose of discipline captures all the major elements that Montessori spoke about in her writings, particularly an emphasis on the community-based development of social consciousness on the part of the child.

---

[20]Dreikurs, *Children: The Challenge,* 84.
[21]Sears, William and Martha, *The Discipline Book* (Boston: Little, Brown and Co., 1995), 6.
[22]Ibid, 7.
[23]Ibid, 225.

The authors give a two-page list of guidelines that can help parents and teachers use appropriate language and techniques to achieve the desired outcome of self-discipline (e.g. connect before you direct, address the child briefly and simply, be positive, give choices, etc.)[24]

One strategy they emphasize is *selective ignoring.*[25] This means ignoring small issues and concentrating on "biggies" or, in other words, learning to pick your battles. If a behavior is not affecting others in the classroom, it is sometimes better not to get in a battle over it.

They also address, in a fairly lengthy discussion, the technique of *time out.*[26] They make it clear that time out seldom works when used as a punishment. Its purpose, in their view, must be to give the child—and adult—time to settle down, reflect and get themselves under control so a fruitful dialogue can take place and a solution acceptable to both sides can be found.

While this re-examination of parental discipline was gaining ground in the public consciousness, there was a corresponding re-thinking of discipline in the context of the school and the classroom. One author who addressed discipline from the viewpoint of an educator was Dr. Jane Nelsen, Ed.D., who wrote the book *Positive Discipline*, offering practical suggestions gleaned from her years as mother and a practicing psychotherapist.[27]

Acknowledging from the beginning her dependence on Dreikurs, Nelsen notes that the goal of positive discipline is to "help children learn self-discipline, responsibility, problem-solving skills, and cooperation,"[28] the same kind of outcomes sought by Montessori. She notes that the concepts about discipline are the same for parents and teachers, and only the setting differs. Furthermore, teachers are generally parents who confront similar issues at home and in school.

She lists as strategies natural and logical consequences, under-standing the goals of misbehavior, kindness and firmness at the same time, mutual respect, class meetings, and encouragement.[29] The

---

[24]Sears, *The Discipline Book,* 162-163.
[25]Ibid, 165.
[26]Ibid, 166-171.
[27]Nelsen, Jane, *Positive Discipline* (New York: Ballantine Books, 1981).
[28]Ibid, 3-4.
[29]Ibid, 6-7.

first two of these are drawn directly from Dreikurs and Adler, while she breaks some new ground with her discussion of class meetings.

Her description of class meetings is very similar to the one we teach in our training course at the Center for Montessori Teacher Education/New York and which will be described in a later chapter.

Some of the same themes show up in more recent publications such as *Discipline with Dignity*, a monograph on positive approaches to discipline from the Association for Supervision and Curriculum Development.[30]

"We define this approach as a set of values on which interventions, strategies, and constructs are built to help children make informed choices to improve their behavior and to make life better for teachers. When that happens, children are so much more likely to learn the content we want to teach, understand why they need to learn it, and comprehend how to use it in constructive ways to improve their lives and the lives of others."[31]

The part about making life better for teachers so children can learn the content they teach is not so consistent with the Montessori approach, but helping children make informed choices and using constructive ways to improve *their* lives resonates more with a Montessori audience. This is an example of how we need to separate expert guidance that works in concert with a Montessori classroom and suggestions that make sense only in traditional settings.

The authors of this study state the same end result of discipline as Montessori: "Our view is that the highest virtue of education is to teach students to be self-responsible and fully functional."[32]

To ensure discipline, they advocate an approach involving prevention (What can be done to prevent problems from occurring?) and action (What can be done when misbehavior occurs to solve the problem without making it worse?).[33]

---

[30]Curwin, Richard L., Allen N. Mendler and Brian D. Mendler, *Discipline with Dignity* (Alexandria, VA : ASCD, 2008).

[31]Ibid, 2.

[32]Ibid, 38.

[33]Ibid, 20.

The first of these goals is to "set up an environment in which discipline problems are prevented,"[34] such as knowing your students, making the classroom a motivating place, teaching responsibility and caring, and establishing clear rules and consequences. This is similar to Montessori's prepared environment.

The action element of this approach depends heavily on the imposition of consequences when inappropriate actions call for them.[35] They go further than Dreikurs in listing not only *natural and logical* consequences, but also what they call *generic* consequences (e.g. reminders or oral warnings), *conventional* consequences (e.g. detention), and *educational* consequences (e.g. teaching a better way to deal with a situation).

While some of these verge on old-fashioned forms of punishment, the authors make a clear distinction between the way the consequences are imposed: "Punishments are done to others. The goal is to achieve the proper amount of misery so that the behavior will not recur... Consequences are what we do to ourselves. The goal is to teach improved decision making in the absence of authority."[36]

All of these authors advocate a form of discipline that maintains respect for the child and echoes Montessori's goal of assisting the child to become self-disciplined. We recommend consulting their work for a more extensive repertoire of effective strategies for classroom discipline.

Conclusion

Without a self-disciplined classroom environment, academic success and motivated students are not possible. A well-disciplined classroom is a pre-requisite for any academic success on the part of the majority of students in the class.

Traditional teachers have known this for ages, and their approach is generally for teachers to take control of the class so there is a minimum of misbehavior and disruption. Montessori urges us to relinquish our

---

[34] Curwin, *Discipline with Dignity*, 46.
[35] Ibid, 65.
[36] Ibid, 83.

control as adults and trust in the ability of the students, to guide them to learn how to be self-disciplined, an approach validated by many non-Montessori authors and experts.

For the Montessori teacher, the practical implication of this research is to rethink the traditional idea of classroom discipline as the teacher's responsibility. We must instead make a renewed commitment to Montessori's goal of assisting each child to develop his or her own self-discipline.

That leads us to the question of what the role of the teacher becomes in this paradigm. Are teachers merely passive observers of this process, or do they have an important role to play? That is the subject of the second chapter.

Chapter 2

Leadership: Redefining the Role of Teacher

The self-discipline of the child described in the previous chapter does not come about without a major contribution of skill and energy on our part as teachers to guide children into the rhythm of a normal Montessori class.

We need to be "in control" of the room without being "controlling." We remain aware of what every student in the room is doing and we intervene when any child seems to be wasting her[1] time or acting in ways that disturb others.

In many education circles, this is called *classroom management.* Once again, we find this traditional language too controlling to match Montessori principles and prefer to call our role one of *classroom leadership.*

This leadership is primarily in the area of helping create a sense of community in the students that will enable them to develop a true sense of self-discipline. It's not our job to control students but to serve as classroom leaders in promoting the values of community.

This means providing a model of community in our own actions. And it means helping students become more aware of that community in their choices and their behavior.

Only in this way can we create conditions that will allow students to become self-disciplined, autonomous learners, acting out of intrinsic motivation.

---

[1] To avoid gender bias and awkward attempts at unisex language, we will alternate references to students as male or female from chapter to chapter. Montessori's own language is tied to her time and is, at times, gender biased to the masculine for the student.

Montessori and Classroom Leadership

"While, in the traditional schools, the teacher sees the immediate behavior of her pupils, knowing that she must look after them and what she has to teach, the Montessori teacher is constantly looking for a child who is not yet there. When she begins work in our schools, she must have a kind of faith that the child will reveal himself through work."[2]

Montessori spoke about the role of the teacher in quite different terms than the usual descriptions of classroom management. Instead of advocating that the teacher maintain control of student behavior, she calls for us to look for the child who exhibits the kind of self-discipline we discussed in the first chapter. We need to wait patiently for the child's behavior to develop through meaningful work.

Montessori compares the teacher-student relationship to one in which "the teacher can find a very good model for her behavior in the way a good valet looks after his master."[3] That's very different than the model of the classroom manager.

Our goal as Montessori teachers is not to maintain control of the classroom at all times but "to be able to say, 'The children are now working as if I did not exist.' "[4]

In *The Secret of Childhood*, Montessori devotes a chapter to the "spiritual preparation of the teacher" and advises her teachers to avoid "being excessively preoccupied with a 'child's tendencies,' with the manner of 'correcting a child's mistakes.'" Instead, she urges them to root out their own defects, particularly any tendencies to anger and pride.

She notes that when we lose our temper in the presence of adults, we feel ashamed; but when we express anger at the behavior of children, "they cannot defend themselves from us, and they accept whatever we tell them. They not only accept abuse, but feel guilty whenever we blame them."[5]

---

[2]Montessori, *Absorbent*, 270.
[3]Ibid, 274.
[4]Ibid, 277.
[5]Montessori, *The Secret of Childhood* (Notre Dame, IN: Fides Publishers,1966), 151.

"A child owes respect to his elders, but adults claim the right to judge and even to offend a child. At their own convenience they direct or even suppress a child's needs, and his protests are regarded as a dangerous and intolerable lack of submission."[6] Montessori, thus, condemns the good old-fashioned classroom management we have come to expect of teachers in traditional settings.

Our real role as teachers, as described in a chapter on teacher preparation of yet another Montessori book, *Spontaneous Activity in Education*, is to become like a *scientist*. "Instead of facility in speech, she has to acquire the power of silence; instead of teaching, she has to observe; instead of the proud dignity of one who claims to be infallible, she assumes the vesture of humility," she wrote in a description of the transformation that must come about for those training to become Montessori teachers.[7]

She goes on to write about developing a capacity for observation that will give us the *"soul of the scientist,"* with all the patience and humility of a true scientist who does not rush to achieve results and is open without any preconceptions to what unfolds on its own.[8]

What makes our science different from the science of an astronomer who studies the stars, a geologist who studies rock formations, or a biologist who studies living organisms is that we are not separate from the object of our study: the emerging spirit of a human being like ourselves. This creates a truly *spiritual* element to our role. "The vision of the teacher should be at once precise like that of the scientist, and spiritual like that of the saint," Montessori wrote.[9]

So, instead of training us to be in control of the classroom and to manage our students' behavior, Montessori seems to be advocating a fairly passive role for us in shaping the behavior of children in our care.

However, Montessori does not intend to leave the child with no guidance from the adult or to permit her to act with absolute liberty. Any society, to function without anarchy, needs laws that limit

---

[6]Montessori, *Secret*, 152.
[7]Montessori, Maria. *Spontaneous Activity in Education: The Advanced Montessori Method* (New York: Schocken Books, 1965), 128.
[8]Ibid,130-134.
[9]Ibid, 137.

individual liberty in the name of the common good or the rights of the collective. The community of the classroom is no different.

"The liberty of the child should have as its *limit* the collective interest," Montessori proclaims.[10] This is a fundamental principle that lies at the heart of her ideas about how a child achieves self-discipline. It is through her inter-actions with the community—of the classroom, in this case—that she discovers a moral code of ethics governing behavior.

And this is where our more active role comes in.

Montessori complains that some of her teachers, tired of her admonitions to give the children liberty, "began to allow the children to do whatever they pleased. I saw children with their feet on the tables, or with their fingers in their noses, and no intervention was made to correct them. I saw others push their companions and I saw dawn on the faces of these an expression of violence, and not the slightest attention on the part of the teacher."[11]

She says that when she saw this happening, she intervened and showed the teachers that they should enforce behavior based on respect for the community, helping children "to discern clearly between good and evil, " without falling into the trap of confusing "good" with immobility or "evil" with activity.

What Montessori observed in these teachers is something that we have experienced frequently, even in otherwise good classrooms. One of the most prevalent mistakes we make is to confuse freedom with license, to be afraid to set limits for children for fear of violating Montessori philosophy or, even worse, for fear of losing our popularity. Limits are necessary to preserve classroom order and respect the rights of everyone in the class.

It's our role to provide *leadership* to help children develop their internal sense of respect for the community. Because of deviations caused by any number of factors, children have to be taught about the rights of the community and led to increased sensitivity to the implications of those rights for their own behavior.

---

[10]Montessori, *Method,* 87.
[11]Ibid, 92-93.

This begins with our own recognition of community in the respect we have for our students and their rights, and in the way we interact with other adults in the classroom and in the school community. We do not always practice what we preach about peaceful collaboration when we deal with co-teachers, assistants, school administrators or parents.

We have to be models in the way we treat others. Our students will recognize petty disagreements in our adult world and our dismissive attitude toward their own rights much quicker than they will pay attention to our lectures on the virtues of community.

It's only if we are providing a positive model of community in our own actions that we can legitimately remind our students of the importance of respecting community in their choices and actions.

Our focus, therefore, should be one of helping children recognize the inherent limits on behavior that come with living in a community like the classroom. Instead of seeking compliance with our own demands, our goal is to encourage self-regulation of behavior on the part of the students in recognition of the reality of the community. This is the foundation for self-discipline, and it is the essence of our leadership role as teachers.

Non-Montessori Views on Community-Based Leadership

Alfie Kohn, whose writings we generally find very compatible with Montessori philosophy, wrote a book[12] that identifies community as the ultimate source of discipline. This approach results in the internal development of the child's own ethical sense and self-disciplined behavior.

He begins by questioning some of the "new discipline" approaches described in Chapter 1, which he generally dismisses as nothing more than a kinder, gentler version of the old-fashioned discipline.[13] While there is danger of crossing that line if we are not paying attention, his critique is arguably too harsh a caricature of approaches that can truly promote a child's self-directed ethical behavior.

---

[12] Kohn, Alfie, *Beyond Discipline: From Compliance to Community* (Alexandria, VA: ASCD, 1996, 2006).
[13] Ibid, 38.

Whatever our view of Kohn's critique of the "new disciplines," we are in total agreement with his argument that the real secret to proper behavior is the development of the child's inner moral and ethical sense in response to her place within the community. He likens this to a constructivist view of behavior that parallels the constructivist theory about learning.

"The only way to help students become ethical people, as opposed to people who merely do what they are told, is to have them construct moral meaning. It is to help them figure out—for themselves and with each other—how one ought to act," he writes.[14]

"It means shifting from eliciting conformity and ending conflict to helping students become active participants in their own social and ethical development."[15] This parallels Montessori's emphasis on children's responsibility for developing themselves.

Kohn argues that creating a true classroom community is the way to sensitize students to the demands of living in society and helping them develop a true internal sense of ethics and responsibility.

"In saying that a classroom or school is a 'community,' then, I mean that it is a place in which students feel cared about and are encouraged to care about each other. They experience a sense of being valued and respected; the children matter to each other and to the teacher. They have come to think in the plural: they feel connected to each other; they are part of an 'us'."[16]

Among Montessori-style community leadership strategies that Kohn endorses elsewhere in the book are "multi-age classrooms and cross-age activities,"[17] "the chance for a teacher to work with the same group of students for more than one year,"[18] and "a teacher who is herself part of a community of adults in the school."[19]

The teacher, in Kohn's view, is someone who must show respect to her students and let them know she cares about them. She is someone

---

[14] Kohn, *Beyond Discipline*, 67.
[15] Ibid, 77.
[16] Ibid, 101.
[17] Ibid, 104.
[18] Ibid, 109.
[19] Ibid, 110.

who encourages connections between students in their work. She is someone who teaches elements of the curriculum with an eye to supporting social and moral growth in her students.[20] This is very much like the kind of teachers Montessori wanted us to be.

While many of the "new discipline" programs cited in Chapter 1 can be helpful to Montessori teachers in developing strategies to effectively provide classroom leadership, Kohn is perhaps closest to Montessori in his approach. He reminds us of two very important principles of Montessori philosophy:

- The ultimate goal is not compliance with adult demands but rather development of the internal ethical sense and morality of the child so that she makes good choices apart from adult manipulation or control. Montessori is always concerned primarily about internal development as the ultimate goal of the educational environment, both in learning content and in social behavior.

- The final criteria for judging the ethics or morality of an action or behavior is its impact on the community. The only real limit on freedom is respect for the community, and this is the only legitimate basis for the classroom leadership strategies employed by teachers to guarantee a calm, orderly and productive classroom. Anything that promotes respect for the community leads to a well-functioning, self-disciplined classroom.

Conclusion

We hope these first two chapters have established that discipline in a Montessori classroom is really about student self-discipline, and classroom management really refers to the teacher's leadership in creating community.

These complementary ideas are the pre-requisites for creating conditions for motivation on the part of the students. Only when these essential factors are firmly established can we address the issue of motivation.

[20]Kohn, *Beyond Discipline,* 109-117.

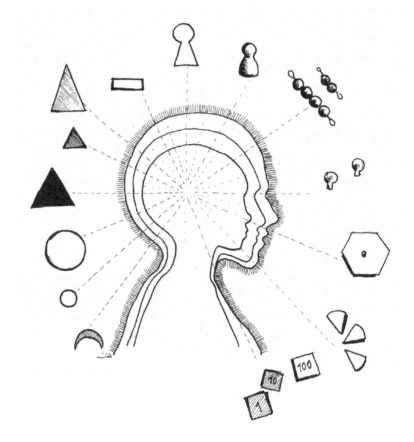

Chapter 3

Auto-Education: The Secret to the Montessori Method

Students are most likely to be motivated in a disciplined environment. Their own self-discipline and our community leadership as teachers create an atmosphere in which students *can* be motivated.

What more is needed for them to be motivated?

For Montessori, the essential element in student motivation is the experience of becoming autonomous learners who are free to develop themselves into the persons they choose to become. The very nature of the enterprise of education, for Montessori, is to support the internal self-development of the child.

Education is not a passive experience of memorizing what a teacher or a textbook tells us. It is an active experience of taking charge of one's own intellectual and psychic development, of growing internally and mentally.

This is the heart and soul of the Montessori method. It is what sets Montessori education radically apart from traditional models of education, either of the blank slate/direct instruction variety or of those based on naturalist/"progressive" theories of education.

It is one of the hallmarks of Montessori education that we encourage children to become ever more independent as they develop toward adulthood. This is true not only in their social and emotional life, but in their academic life as well.

Montessori, once again ahead of her time, places the responsibility for learning squarely on the shoulders of the students, relegating us to a supporting role in the teaching/learning exchange. We can teach all day, but it's the job of the students to learn—and we can't do it for them. This, we will see, is very much in line with the thinking of those who call themselves constructivist educators in today's world.

Autonomy in Montessori Philosophy

"The fundamental rights of man are those of his own 'formation,' free from obstacles, free from slavery, and free to draw from his environment the means required for his development." [1]

To understand Montessori's theories about autonomy, we must begin with her concept of the nature of the *work* of the child. Montessori draws a contrast between the work of the adult, geared to an external product, and the work of the child, whose goal is an internal product.

Adults work to create something—a car, a book, a service, a work of art—with value to others; they generally do this in the quickest way possible, investing the least possible amount of energy and resources to get the most valuable outcome, something we identify as *productivity*.

The product of children's work, she maintained, was the development of their inner life or psyche, moving them toward becoming the adult person they choose to be in life. In any activity, producing an external result quickly or with little effort is less important than maximizing the amount of internal development that takes place.

She calls children "spiritual (psychic) embryos"[2] at birth, tasked with developing their inner life through every activity and work that they undertake. She viewed this transformation from child to adult as the "work" of the child, something to be accomplished through those four planes or stages of development that she spoke about to reach true adulthood. And she insisted that this was the work of the child, not of the adult-parent-teacher.

"Although he cannot share in the work of adults, he has his own difficult and important task to perform, that of producing a man...It is solely from a child that a man is formed... 'The child is the father of

---

[1]Montessori, *Spontaneous,* 197.
[2]Montessori, *Absorbent,* 68.

the man.'"[3] Later, she adds, "... just as the embryo becomes a child and a child becomes a man, so the human personality is formed through its own efforts."[4] This is the rationale for her insistence on autonomy for the child in his educational life.

Montessori is very clear in proclaiming that the task of the child is one that only he can accomplish. In many of her writings and lectures, she railed against adults who would interfere with the natural development of the child. "Woe to us, when we believe ourselves responsible for matters that do not concern us, and delude ourselves with the idea that we are perfecting things that will perfect themselves quite independently of us!"[5]

In other words, Montessori believed in what she came to call "auto-education," or the ability of children to educate themselves and develop their human personality by their own activity. She called this one of the fundamental rights of man, the freedom to develop their own identity—the true purpose of education—without interference or hindrance from any source outside themselves.

So, just as she advocated self-discipline, she calls for auto-education. But, like discipline, this does not mean that we are to abandon children and expect them to fend for themselves without any assistance. We play an important role in allowing the child to auto-educate. In fact, this is the way Montessori defines the task of education—to assist the child in achieving this self-development.

The way this is accomplished is through providing the child with a properly *prepared environment*, a fundamental concept in Montessori theory and practice.

"The first aim of the prepared environment is, as far as it is possible, to render the growing child independent of the adult,"[6] her biographer summarized her thoughts on the subject.

When we were building our own school in rural Georgia, the very perceptive architect who was helping us plan the building mentioned that designing a Montessori classroom was different from

---

[3]Montessori, *Secret*, 35.
[4]Ibid.
[5]Montessori, *Spontaneous*, 6.
[6]Standing, E.M., *Maria Montessori: Her Life and Work* (New York: New American Library, 1957), 267.

other schools he had designed. He noted that there is no architectural center of authority in a Montessori classroom, no designated place for the teacher to preside. The very design of the room speaks to the dispersed authority of self-government.

When a visitor enters any Montessori classroom, it is sometimes difficult for them to find the teacher. More often than not, we are off in a corner working with a small group of students or an individual child.

This central notion of a prepared environment is a very rich concept, full of meaning for anyone who studies Montessori's writings. To isolate just a few of the implications of this term, a prepared environment includes the presence of Montessori materials, a multi-age classroom, and a special adult-child relationship.

A combination of these factors leads to an environment in which the child can auto-educate. "It is therefore necessary that the environment should contain the means of auto-education." [7]

The Montessori materials are a major element in the prepared environment. The materials not only contribute to the ability of students to self-discipline, as discussed in Chapter 1, but they offer them a means to auto-educate as well, creating the possibility of turning them into life-long autonomous learners.

Developed first in her work with special needs children (borrowing heavily from Jean Marc Gaspard Itard and Edouard Seguin, two French physician-educators considered pioneers in the special education movement), Montessori eventually used these materials with a general school population and found they served a different purpose: "...the same didactic material used with deficients makes education possible, while with normal children it provokes auto-education." [8]

To emphasize this point, Montessori makes an important distinction between using materials as visual aids for the teacher and using them as learning tools for the students. Didactic materials are used in a traditional classroom primarily as "an aid to the teacher in making hisexplanations comprehensible to a collective class listening passively to him." [9]

---

[7] Montessori, *Spontaneous*, 72.
[8] Montessori, *Method*, 169.
[9] Montessori, *Spontaneous*, 85.

In a Montessori class, by contrast, they are "means of development," they promote "the psychic evolution of the child; and their aim is not to give mere instruction; they represent the means which induce a spontaneous interpretation of the internal energies."[10]

So the materials belong primarily to the students for their own work. They can be used as teaching aids in a lesson, but their primary role is to give students tools with which to develop their inner selves. This is why they are a means of auto-education.

When we give beautiful presentations with the materials and believe we have given the children all the knowledge they need, we have jumped from first period (presentation) to third period (assessment). We must seduce the children into second period work (practice), the most important step in the learning process for Montessori.

"Between 'understanding' because another person seeks to impress upon us the explanation of a thing by speech, and 'understanding' the thing of ourselves, there is an immeasurable distance; the two are comparable to the impression made in soft wax…and the form chiseled in the marble by an artist, as his creation."[11]

There are qualities in the design of Montessori materials that allow children to auto-educate, to explore and discover things for themselves.

When a lower elementary student uses a simple material like a fingerboard to learn his addition or subtraction facts, he is auto-educating, albeit in a very simple way. This is significantly different from being given a list of combinations with the answers already provided and told to memorize them. Instead, a student finds the answer himself to a given combination by moving his fingers to the intersecting number to get the right answer.

When an upper elementary student uses the yellow area materials to find the formula for the area of a triangle, we don't tell him the formula. Instead, the student manipulates the cut pieces of the triangle, transforming them into the shape of a rectangle. He then compares the bases and heights of the triangle and rectangle, and figures out *for himself* the formula of half the base times the height. This is real auto-

---

[10]Montessori, *Spontaneous*, 86.
[11]Ibid, 215.

education, using the materials to replicate the discovery of the formula the way the Greeks did thousands of years ago.

Montessori designed her materials to give children tools to help them focus and concentrate for *self-discipline* as well as to explore and to take charge of their own learning for *auto-education*. This approach is totally different from that used in traditional education.

A multi-age classroom is another aspect of the prepared environment that promotes autonomy and independence among the students. A classroom with children of different ages establishes a community in ways that a single-age classroom cannot do and more realistically mirrors the multi-age communities of home and adult work place.

It encourages the emergence of leadership qualities among the older children and gives younger children role models to follow, other than the adults in the room. This takes advantage of the natural motivation that younger children have to imitate fellow students who are a year or two older than themselves.

More to the point, multi-age classrooms promote independent learning as elementary students spend much of their day collaborating, without teacher intervention. This creates a synergy in their work that carries them well beyond what they could accomplish alone with a workbook or textbook. Because only a year or two ago they struggled with the same problems, older students can help younger ones, often more effectively than adult teachers.

A third important element in creating autonomous learners is the interaction between teachers and students. If we spend most of our time controlling behavior and giving direct instruction, our classrooms become traditional ones rather than Montessori environments for auto-education.

On the other hand, if we remain constantly aware of our student's rights to develop themselves internally, we will support that growth. No effective Montessori teacher will obstruct the desirable outcomes of self-control, self-discipline and self-learning that are essential for their students' motivation to learn.

Non-Montessori Literature about Auto-Education

While there is not an extensive body of literature that makes autonomous learning one of the principal goals of education, the idea has been around in one form or another for a long time. Jean Piaget, a contemporary of Montessori, had a view of education that promoted autonomy and activity on the part of the student, the foundations of a later approach to pedagogy called *constructivism*.[12]

Piaget, a Swiss psychologist whose principal work involved the epistemology of cognitive development, nevertheless wrote about the implications of his findings for education, and his influence in educational circles is immeasurable. It's interesting to note that he not only knew of Montessori's work and agreed with many of her ideas, but he served as president of the Swiss Montessori Society.

Piaget came to many conclusions that are very similar to those of Montessori:

- Children think in a different way than adults do,

- Development follows a specific sequence of stages,

- Education is more about developing the powers of the mind than the transmission of specific content,

- Education must address not only intellectual skills but the holistic development of the child,

- The child must have an active role in education, and

- Activity is the only way to allow for the child's spontaneous mental development.[13]

The authors of *Constructivist Early Education* entitle the chapter about Piaget, "Piaget's Theory and Education: Forming the Mind, Not Just Furnishing It."[14]

---

[12]DeVries, Rheta and Lawrence Kohlberg, *Constructivist Early Education: Overview and Comparison with Other Programs* (Washington, DC: National Association for the Education of Young Children, 1990).
[13]Ibid, 262-264. Ginsburg, Herbert and Sylvia Opper, *Piaget's Theory of Intellectual Development: An Introduction* (Englewood Cliffs, NJ: Prentice Hall, 1969), 218 ff.
[14]DeVries, *Constructivist*, 17.

They quote Piaget: "If the child's thought is qualitatively different from our own, then the principal aim of education is to form its intellectual and moral reasoning power. And since that power cannot be formed from outside, the question is to find the most suitable methods and environment to help the child constitute itself."[15]

What's particularly noteworthy about this quote from Piaget is the conclusion that the intellectual and moral development of the child is something that cannot be done by the adult, and that our role is to provide the proper environment to allow the child to develop himself— ideas directly related to Montessori's views on auto-education and the role of the prepared environment.

Piaget, in his theory of knowledge building, argued that learning is not just about the environment (*stimulus*) affecting the learner (*organism*), but that there is a two-way interaction between the learner and his environment.

Piaget specifies this interaction with the terms *assimilation*, "where the organism acts on the stimulus and interprets it in terms of previous knowledge," and *accommodation*, "where the stimulus acts on the organism and previous knowledge is modified."[16]

This is the basis of the whole theory of constructivism, which holds that "the knower actively constructs knowledge,"[17] by internally merging pre-existing knowledge with some new piece of information.

The existing literature about constructivism indicates that there is still considerable dispute about exactly how to define it, the different forms that it takes, and how it is applied to specific subjects. But each source reveals a common starting point—knowledge is something *constructed* by the interaction of the learner with his environment. This is auto-education.

Modern writers express the validity of this concept in their own words. According to Virginia Richardson, a University of Michigan specialist in teacher education theories, "The general sense of constructivism is that it is a theory of learning or meaning making, that

---

[15]Devries, *Constructivist*, 19. Citing Jean Piaget, *Science of Education and the Psychology of the Child* (New York: Viking, 1969), 159-160.

[16]DeVries, *Constructivist*, 8.

[17]Ibid.

individuals create their own understandings on the basis of interaction between what they already know and believe and ideas and knowledge with which they come into contact."[18]

And Dr. Ronald Bonnstetter of the University of Nebraska writes, "Constructivism, reduced to its most basic elements, is simply a learning or meaning-making theory. This theory proposes that people create their own meaning and understanding, combining what they already know and believe to be true with new experiences with which they are confronted."[19]

However it is defined, constructivism gives the child an active role in developing his own knowledge—corresponding, in broad terms, to Montessori's auto-education.

DeVries and Kohlberg contrast constructivism with other approaches to education they define as *romantic* and *cultural transmission.*

The romantic approach, epitomized in the "open school" movement of A. S. Neill's Summerhill, views education as the "unfolding of innate, pre-patterned, predetermined stages"[20] with little adult intervention. The cultural transmission approach, which remains the prevalent model used in public and private schools throughout the country, can be traced back to John Locke's view of children as "blank slates" on which teachers write information and B.F. Skinner's stimulus-response learning, aka behaviorism.[21]

As we've seen, Montessori rejects both of those approaches to learning in favor of her theory of autonomy and auto-education. Constructivism, which embraces the views of Piaget and John Dewey, also rejects these other two approaches as inadequate to describe a vision of the learner as active, substituting instead what they call a cognitive-developmental view of learning.

DeVries and Kohlberg even dedicate a chapter of their book to comparing Montessori with their idea of constructivism. Despite some

---

[18]Richardson, V., "Constructivist Pedagogy," *Teachers College Record,* Vol. 105, No. 9 (December 2003): 1623-1640.

[19]Bonnstetter, Ronald, "A Constructivist Approach to Science Teacher Preparation." http://nerds.unl.edu/pages/preser/sec/articles/construct.html.

[20]DeVries, *Constructivist,* 3.

[21]Ibid, 5.

differences, they conclude that Montessori is more like Piaget and Dewey than either the romantic or cultural transmission models.

The bottom line is that Montessori, particularly at the elementary level, is much more similar to constructivism than the prevalent teacher-dominated, direct instruction, cultural transmission model of education. Constructivism generally supports Montessori's ideas of autonomy and auto-education.

Conclusion

Montessori's theory about motivation begins with the belief that children become self-disciplined through engagement with work that develops them internally. They become autonomous learners through use of the materials and other elements in the prepared environment.

Our role, within that theory, is twofold: to provide classroom leadership in promoting community to support the student's self-discipline; and to prepare the environment to support the student's auto-education.

Self-discipline and auto-education are the foundation for Montessori's advocacy of intrinsic motivation over extrinsic motivation, a clearly stated point of view that we will examine in the next chapter.

Chapter 4

Motivation: Intrinsic vs. Extrinsic

Now, we turn to Montessori's explicit ideas about motivation itself, with a discussion of intrinsic motivation. This concept is closely aligned to the issue of autonomy and auto-education, covered in the last chapter.

If motivation is encouraged externally, through rewards and punishments, this does little to promote autonomy; instead, it promotes a dependency of the child on the adult for direction to action. On the other hand, if motivation is intrinsic, or coming from within the child, it supports auto-education.

This is the basis for Montessori's advocacy of intrinsic motivation. Autonomous learners are, by definition, intrinsically motivated. Students cannot auto-educate unless they are driven by their own internal engine, and their smiles are the outward sign that that engine is functioning.

Conversely, auto-education feeds intrinsic motivation. The more students become autonomous learners, the more intrinsically motivated they are.

The two are complementary ideas in Montessori theory, in a sort of chicken-and-egg way. One does not come before the other—they occur simultaneously in the experience of the students.

We will find that Montessori's ideas about intrinsic motivation are heavily supported by modern research. This research shows that intrinsic motivators stimulate love of learning much more effectively than extrinsic motivators.

Montessori and Intrinsic Motivation

> *"Prizes and punishments are, if I may be allowed the expression, the bench of the soul, the instrument of slavery for the spirit... he who accomplishes a truly human work, he who does something really great and victorious, is never spurred to his task by those trifling attractions called by the name of 'prizes,' nor by the fear of those petty ills which we call 'punishments'."*[1]

In the debate over the most effective motivators, Montessori is unequivocal in her rejection of extrinsic rewards and punishments.

She noted that after repeatedly experimenting with rewards of good behavior badges or even offering students candy for their work, they responded either with indifference or outright rejection. She came to the point where "we gave up either punishing or rewarding the children."[2]

Instead, she argues that the best motivator for children is their experience of internal growth when they are deeply engaged in work. This creates pleasure and the desire to do more work.

"Man, disciplined through liberty," she wrote, "begins to desire the true and only prize which will never belittle or disappoint him—the birth of human power and liberty within that inner life of his from which his activities must spring."[3]

Montessori uses the term *horme* to describe the internal drive of the child, named for the Greek goddess of energetic activity.

"The child's conquest of independence begins with his first introduction to life. While he is developing, he perfects himself and overcomes every obstacle that he finds in his path. A vital force is active within him, and this guides his efforts towards their goal. It is a force called *'horme'* by Sir Percy Nunn."[4]

In a footnote, she compares this driving energy of the child to Henri Bergson's *élan vital,* the force this French philosopher and evolutionist

---

[1]Montessori, *Method,* 23.
[2]Montessori, *Secret,* 123.
[3]Montessori, *Method,* 101.
[4]Montessori, *Absorbent,* 90. Nunn was a British educator of the early 20th century.

credits for the survival tendency of every species and the energy that advances the very process of evolution.

Later, she writes, "there are theories which suggest that man's will proceeds from a great universal power (*horme*), and that this universal force is not physical, but is the force of life itself in the process of evolution. It drives every form of life irresistibly toward evolution, and from it come the impulses to action."[5]

She argues that it is this internal force that drives the will of the child toward the third level of obedience and, ultimately, motivation for her actions.

The Modern Literature about Intrinsic Motivation

There is a large body of research and literature supporting the goal of intrinsic motivation that has developed and spread its influence in recent decades.

As educators began to question the effectiveness of behaviorism and other systems of rewards and punishments—about the same time that spanking was being discouraged—proponents of intrinsic motivation began to emerge with a replacement theory for behavior modification.

Behavior modification is a product of the theories of the renowned psychologist B.F. Skinner, who turned manipulation into a real science that came to dominate school practice throughout the United States. Rewards and punishments were elevated to the role of prime motivators designed to get children to do what adults wanted them to do.

One of the first to challenge this approach was Edward Deci,[6] who studied psychology as an undergraduate at Hamilton College in Clinton, NY. Through a stroke of irony, this college was also Skinner's alma mater.

Deci recalls that he began questioning the benefits of behaviorism when he reflected on the fact that very young children seem to learn with enthusiasm and intensity, only to lose their drive gradually as they grow older. Over years of research, begun in 1969 as a doctoral student

---

[5]Montessori, *Absorbent,* 248.
[6]Deci, Edward. *Why We Do What We Do* (New York, NY: Penguin Books, 1995), 19.

at Carnegie-Mellon University in Pittsburgh, he eventually concluded that growing up in a system of rewards and punishments conditions them out of their natural love of learning.

"Behaviorist dogma assumes that there is no inherent motivation to learn, but this does not square with the fact that young children—in preschools and at home—ceaselessly explore and manipulate the objects they encounter. They challenge themselves to be competent, apparently just for the enjoyment of doing it...they are *intrinsically motivated* to learn."[7]

"In 1969, I had the fleeting—and surely blasphemous—thought that maybe all the rewards, rules and regimentation that were so widely used to motivate schoolchildren were themselves the villains," he wrote, "promoting not an excited state of learning but a sad state of apathy."[8]

In the remainder of the book, he describes the rigorous experiments that he and colleagues conducted to determine whether this hypothesis was true. Using an experimental paradigm, he asked groups of subjects to perform a variety of tasks, with one group receiving extrinsic rewards and the second group no rewards. Then, the experiment's subjects were left on their own to see what would happen. In every case, those who got the rewards abandoned the task, while those who didn't receive the rewards continued to play with the puzzle or other task "just for fun."[9]

He deduced that rewards and punishments, over the long term, actually undermine performance. Intrinsic motivation, by contrast, is a long-term stimulus to learning that produces many desirable outcomes.

"Intrinsic motivation is associated with richer experience, better conceptual understanding, greater creativity, and improved problem solving, relative to external controls. Not only do controls undermine intrinsic motivation and engagement with activities but—and here is a bit of bad news for people focused on the bottom line—they have clearly detrimental effects on performance of any tasks that require creativity, conceptual understanding, or flexible problem solving."[10]

---

[7]Deci, *Why We Do,* 20.
[8]Ibid, 22.
[9]Ibid, 25.
[10]Ibid, 51.

In many places throughout the book, Deci makes the point that motivation is not something done *to* the child, but rather it must be something done *by* the child. He likens it to a *life force[11]*, similar to Montessori's use of *horme,* and he pays homage to the prepared environment by noting, "we view human behavior and experience in terms of the dialectic between the person and the environment."[12]

Finally, Deci recognizes the need for limits to actions in light of their impact on society, mirroring Montessori's description of limits to freedom. "To advocate autonomy does not mean to call for self-indulgence, because *being truly oneself* involves accepting responsibility for the well-being of others."[13]

Alfie Kohn is another author who examines motivation in a book entitled *Punished by Rewards*.[14] Unlike Deci, Kohn does not do original research, but he gathers the findings of other researchers and compiles them into a coherent, concise, and convincing argument for his point of view, in this case, the superiority of intrinsic motivation.

He notes that the pervasive influence of behaviorism "reflects a thoroughly American sensibility"[15] of dedication to the bottom line.

In the field of education, we have turned this into a way of life based on an elaborate system of rewards. "To induce students to learn, we present stickers, stars, certificates, awards, trophies, membership in elite societies, and above all, grades. If the grades are good enough, some parents then hand out bicycles or cards or cash, thereby offering what are, in effect, rewards for rewards."[16]

Like Deci, Kohn recounts that he first questioned behaviorism in an Introduction to Psychology course that he nearly failed because he insisted on making a mockery of the practice of training rats to press a lever for food. He wrote a parody for the school paper that claimed a 100 percent success rate in conditioning rats to avoid pressing lever

[11]Deci, *Why We Do,* 81.
[12]Ibid, 83.
[13]Ibid,103.
[14]Kohn, Afie. *Punished by Rewards: The Trouble with Gold Stars, Incentive Plans, A's, Praise and Other Bribes* (Boston: Houghton Mifflin, 1993).
[15]Ibid, 9.
[16]Ibid, 11.

B more than once by dropping a three-hundred-pound anvil on them when that lever was chosen.[17]

By the time he moved to Cambridge—hometown of Skinner—Kohn invited the distinguished professor to visit the classroom where he was teaching, and he even interviewed Skinner twice to write a profile of him for a magazine.

But Kohn had trouble with Skinner's theories, which he calls *dehumanizing* and *demeaning* because they make a giant leap from experiments with pigeons and rats to human behavior.[18]

However, his more fundamental objection is that even benign sounding rewards have a dark side. "... one of the most important (and unsettling) things we can recognize is that the real choice for us is not between rewards and punishments but between either version of behavioral manipulation, on the one hand, and an approach that does not rely on control, on the other."[19]

Rewards—no differently than punishments—are means of control of one person over another. They create an unequal status in power between the two and ultimately benefit the more powerful party, who decides and presents the reward.

What is even worse, they don't work in the long run. If the effectiveness of rewards is to be judged by their ability "to produce lasting change, the research suggests that they fail miserably."[20] To back this up, Kohn cites numerous studies on everything from weight loss programs, to quitting smoking, to using seat belts.

In the long run, he argues, rewards are counterproductive, producing an addictive dependence that leads to abandonment of the behavior once the rewards are removed. For this, he cites decades of research beginning in the 1960s up to the present, from people like Janet Spence (University of Texas), Barry Schwartz (Swarthmore College), Teresa Amabile (Harvard Business School), Mark Lepper (Stanford University), Morton Deutsch (Columbia University), Ann Boggiano

---

[17] Kohn, *Punished,* xi.
[18] Ibid, 24-25.
[19] Ibid, 26.
[20] Ibid, 37.

and Marty Barrett (University of Colorado), Kenneth McGraw (University of Mississippi), as well as Deci and his colleague at the University of Rochester, Richard Ryan.

What all these researchers found in their experiments and studies is the surprising and counter-intuitive outcome that rewards actually undermine performance in the long run. Kohn concludes, "Even assuming we have no ethical reservations about manipulating other people's behavior to get them to do what we want, the plain truth is that this strategy is likely to backfire."[21]

Kohn lists a number of reasons why he believes this to be the case, beginning with the argument that rewards and punishments are essentially the same in the way they control others, even if one does it more by seduction. In a typical Kohn zinger, he writes: "The question is not whether more flies can be caught with honey than with vinegar, but *why* the flies are being caught in either case—and how this feels to the fly."[22]

Other reasons he gives for the failure of rewards is that they rupture relationships by pitting participants against each other, they ignore the reasons for behavior, they discourage risk-taking and encourage meeting only minimum requirements. Most importantly, they change the way people feel about what they do, shifting the emphasis to the means and taking the focus off the end.

"Do this and you'll get that!"—Kohn's shorthand mantra for the behaviorist approach—automatically devalues "this" and shifts the focus to "that," he argues.[23]

Kohn even advocates against the most innocuous, positive, well-intentioned form of rewards—praise—dedicating an entire chapter to the subject. Praise has all the drawbacks of other forms of rewards, such as being a subtle way of getting students to do what we want and creating an addictive dependence on praise that eventually backfires in the long run when behavior is expected in the absence of praise.

---

[21] Kohn, *Punished*, 47.
[22] Ibid, 52.
[23] Ibid, 76.

In addition, Kohn argues that praise for tasks that aren't particularly difficult may be interpreted as saying we don't think the person receiving the praise is very smart, that praise invites a low-risk strategy to avoid failure in the future and, most importantly, it reduces interest in the task itself, undermining intrinsic motivation.[24]

Kohn, however, takes pains to make clear he is not against any positive feedback—just not in the form of empty praise. "I distinguish between various forms of positive feedback: on the one hand, straightforward information about how well someone has done a task," he wrote, "or encouragement that leaves the recipient feeling a sense of self-determination; on the other hand, verbal rewards that feel controlling, make one dependent on someone else's approval, and in general prove to be no less destructive than other extrinsic motivators."[25]

In other words, when a child presents us with a very child-like drawing, it's inappropriate to gush, "Wow! You're really a great artist!" But it would be appropriate to say something like, "I really like the way those bright colors make your painting attractive and fun."

We should praise the work, not the person. Make praise specific rather than general. Don't be phony. And avoid praise that sets up competition. This last point leads Kohn to warn us away from using an old favorite, "I like the way Susie is sitting quietly and ready for circle."

Daniel Pink is one of the latest authors to promote the idea of intrinsic motivation. His book *Drive*,[26] like Kohn's, is a collection of years of research by others on the origin and nature of effective motivation.

He begins with a nod to the work of Deci and Harry Harlow, professor of psychology at the University of Wisconsin. In the 1940s, Harlow was already using behavioral studies to show that monkeys and other primates were motivated not only by biological needs and rewards and punishments, but also by a form of intrinsic reward from the joy in the task itself.

While most of Kohn's work tends to focus on schools and parenting, Pink's orientation is primarily the business world. He opens Chapter

---

[24]Kohn, *Punished*, 98-101.
[25]Ibid, 96.
[26]Pink, Daniel, *Drive: The Surprising Truth About What Motivates Us* (New York: Riverhead Books, 2009).

1 with an imaginary story of an economist trying to predict in 1995 which would be more successful: an encyclopedia produced by one of the leading companies in the world, Microsoft, with paid professionals crafting thousands of articles to be assembled for sale on CD-ROMs or online; or an encyclopedia created by tens of thousands of hobbyists, who don't get a penny for the countless hours they volunteer writing an online encyclopedia that is free to anyone who wants to use it. Microsoft pulled the plug on MSN Encarta in 2009, while Wikipedia has become the largest and most popular encyclopedia in the world.[27]

He talks about three versions of motivation: Motivation 1.0, which was all about human survival in largely hostile environments in pre-historic days, before the complexities of societies; Motivation 2.0, the "carrots and sticks" approach that has dominated society for as long as there have been societies; and Motivation 3.0, the latest upgrade in motivation which recognizes the power of intrinsic motivation.

In addition to the Wikipedia example, Deci cites other "open source" products produced by all volunteer staffs and offered free to anybody who wants to use them, such as the web browser Firefox, which has 150 million users around the world; Linux, a software system that now powers one in four corporate servers; Apache, a Web server software that has a 52 percent share of the corporate market; and countless other open source projects, from cookbooks, to textbooks, to car design, to legal briefs, to stock photos, to medical research, to credit unions, to beer.[28]

Behavioral scientists often divide what we do on the job into two categories, called *algorithmic* and *heuristic* tasks. The algorithmic task involves following a set of established instructions down a single pathway to the product; a heuristic task requires one to experiment and devise a novel solution. The first works best with Motivation 2.0 carrots and sticks, while the latter works best with Motivation 3.0.

Pink cites the findings of the consultant firm McKinsey & Co. that estimated that, in the United States, "only 30 percent of job growth nowcomes from algorithmic work, while 70 percent comes from

[27]Pink, *Drive*, 15-17.
[28]Ibid, 22.

heuristic work. A key reason: Routine work can be outsourced or automated; artistic, empathic, non-routine work generally cannot."[29]

He reviews the same literature compiled by Kohn, and later research as well, to document that Motivation 2.0, with its dependence on rewards and punishments, actually undermines motivation in the long run. He lists the seven deadly sins of external rewards: they extinguish intrinsic motivation, they diminish performance, they crush creativity, they crowd out good behavior, they encourage cheating and unethical behavior, they become addictive, and they foster short-term thinking.[30]

Pink cites several business models that have proven the worth—and monetary profit—of promoting intrinsic motivation instead. ROWE, developed by two Best Buy executives, creates a "results only work environment," in which employees show up when they want and just need to get their assigned work done—how they want, when they want, and even where they want. Companies like a software firm in Charlottesville, VA, have turned that system into a profitable business where employees are less likely to jump to another job for even a $20,000 increase in salary.[31]

Another model is "Fed Ex" days, where employees are given a day off from their regular duties in return for producing something entirely on their own, with overnight delivery of the idea. The 3M company turned this idea into a plan to give employees 15 percent of their time to work on projects of their own choosing, and *post-its* were one of the wildly successful products that emerged. *Gmail* was the creation of a Google employee using the 20 percent free time offered by that corporate giant.

"The science shows that the secret to high performance isn't our biological drive or our reward-and-punishment drive, but our third drive—our deep-seated desire to direct our own lives, to extend and expand our abilities, and to live a life of purpose," Pink concludes.[32]

The intrinsic motivation described by Deci, Kohn and Pink is the type of motivation that Montessori wanted to promote in classrooms. She did no extensive scientific experiments to come to that conclusion;

[29]Pink, *Drive,* 30.
[30]Ibid, 59.
[31]Ibid, 86-87.
[32]Ibid, 145.

her science consisted in years of observing the contented smiles that spread across the faces of children as they completed some piece of work and, in the process, grew internally.

Conclusion

Clearly it should be our goal to have intrinsically motivated students in our classrooms and all that we have discussed to this point can be helpful in bringing this about. This includes support of student self-discipline, leadership in creating community, encouragement of auto-education on the part of the student, and avoidance of anything that would shift motivation from intrinsic back to extrinsic motivators.

These four chapters are an attempt to summarize the principles and basic theory behind Montessori's ideas about motivation. Obviously, this begs for practical strategies to implement the theory and assure that students are genuinely motivated. That is the focus of the second part of this book.

The practical suggestions included in Part 2 are based first of all on guidance from Montessori herself, on our experience in implementing Montessori theory in our own classrooms, and in observing successful teachers in classrooms we have visited. It also draws heavily from some of these modern experts in the field who offer their own strategies to promote motivation in students.

Part 2
The Practical Side

Strategies for Promoting Intrinsic Motivation

Chapter 5

The Fundamentals: Implementation of Theory

So, we've tried to figure out Montessori's theory about motivation in Part 1. And we've examined that theory against modern authors, both to see whether the principles involved are valid and to gain further insights into what is implied by the theory.

Now it's time to discuss some practical ways to implement the theory.

A first set of strategies will come from an examination of our classroom practice in the light of the Montessori principles outlined above. We need to determine whether we are taking care of the fundamentals—supporting self-discipline and auto-education in our students, and providing leadership in creating community. Only then can we hope to motivate our students in the way Montessori envisioned.

However, that might not do the job as effectively as we might hope. There are strategies we can employ that are suggested by modern experts in the field, based on extensive research on the subject in the half century since Montessori's death. To ignore that body of knowledge would be a mistake, depriving our students of practices that could help them become intrinsically motivated.

Many of our students achieve intrinsic motivation on most days simply because of our Montessori classroom practices. But there are others who struggle to ever get excited about learning, and we may need to offer something more for them.

All of our students, both those who seem to thrive naturally in a Montessori environment and those whom we struggle to reach, can benefit from the suggestions about motivation that have been developed in the light of modern scientific research.

Before we consider those suggestions from modern research, let's begin our discussion of practical strategies with some Montessori fundamentals, to make sure we are maximizing those important Montessori principles we discussed in Part 1.

There are some typical Montessori tactics that we can use to support an atmosphere of classroom discipline and to encourage auto-education among our students.

Leadership Strategies to Support Self-Discipline

One of our main jobs in the classroom is to develop practices that build community consciousness and provide support for student self-discipline in the context of that community.

If the limit to individual freedom is the collective good, then it makes sense to spend time and energy building a sense of community. There are a number of procedures that we have incorporated into our own classrooms or observed in other schools that we have visited in the course of our work. The following is a list of some helpful practices:

• Community Building Activities

We typically begin each school year with community building activities designed to welcome new students into the class and to form a bond of mutual respect and collaboration with all the members of the class. This is an important investment of time that pays off in dividends the whole school year. There is a more unified feeling of being a class community, there is more tolerance of differences and idiosyncrasies, and there is a greater spirit of cooperation and recognition of each other's strengths and weaknesses.

This can consist in fun activities to allow everyone to get to know each other's names (e.g. passing a ball around as you call out the name of the person you toss it to next, having each student introduce the person sitting next to them, or attaching your own name to the first letter of a favorite food); ice-breaker style games that allow everyone to just be silly (e.g. having each student pick a tag with a barnyard animal written on it and finding your group of fellow animals by making appropriate animal sounds, putting the name of a famous person on each person's back and trying to guess who it is on your own back with yes or no questions to others in the room).

We also use affirmation sessions where students pick out something they like about themselves or the person sitting next to them in circle, so they get to know more about each other and learn to value each other's unique qualities; trust building games (e.g. leading a blindfolded peer around a temporary obstacle course); or group problem solving games (e.g. lining up in order of height or some other quality without talking).

This might appear to be a waste of student time that should be devoted instead to academics. But the relationships of students to each other is critical to their emotional stability and their ability to focus on academic work. Whatever time is spent at the beginning of the school year—or periodically throughout the year—on building community lays a necessary foundation for calm and peaceful academic work.

• Overnight Field Trips

One practice that has proven effective in creating a sense of community is the use of over-night field trips, particularly in the early part of the school year.

For lower elementary students at our school, this usually consisted of a one-day field trip that lasted longer than the usual school day, ending with a Friday night sleepover at the school—in familiar territory for the novices in the group. Then they could be picked up by their parents on Saturday morning. For upper elementary students, we usually did a two- or three-night fall trip to some outdoor education site within our own state.

These trips not only serve a direct educational purpose but they give the students an opportunity to learn how to take care of themselves and their classmates without the presence of their parents. This boosts their independence, self-confidence, and sense of community with each other outside the classroom context.

• Grace and Courtesy Lessons

We usually give "grace and courtesy lessons" at the primary level, but even older students need to be taught how to interact in a community.

There is ample opportunity for some of these lessons at both lower and upper elementary levels. Children need to be taught many social skills, including how to greet visitors to the classroom, how to prepare a place setting for lunch, how to write thank you letters to parent volunteers, and how to act appropriately when out on a field trip or in other public settings.

Essential to maintaining a community is a classroom job list. This assigns rotating tasks to individual students including such chores as taking care of pets, plants, and the cleanliness of different areas of the classroom. These jobs reinforce the idea that everyone has responsibilities in a community. In addition they help students to be self-reliant and capable of maintaining order and cleanliness in the classroom environment.

As teachers, we have to give the initial lessons on how to do each job. Then students pass on to each other the routines as they rotate the responsibilities periodically.

• Classroom Rules or Rights

In most of our classrooms lists of rules or rights are posted prominently, highlighting the concept that individual liberty must take into account the rights of others. These lists should be student-generated if they are to promote self-discipline.

At the lower elementary level, they might include statements like "Everyone has a right to work without being disturbed," and "Everyone has a right to choose the place where they work." At the upper elementary level, they might consist of a real bill of rights focused on more emotional issues for the class, including pledges such as "Everyone has a right to feel safe (from bullying, etc.)," and "Everyone has a right to be included."

Such lists vary greatly from class to class, and it is not necessary for them to be comprehensive in the sense that they include every expectation for classroom behavior. It is important only that they represent an acknowledgment on the part of everyone in the class that there are limits to individual freedom and actions must be based on the common good or the needs of living in community.

To signify their acceptance of these rights and rules, all students and teachers sign the final document that is then posted on the wall. There is no doubt that this student-generated list inspires good classroom behavior much more effectively than rules we impose unilaterally on students.

• Peace Education

"Peace Education" is at the heart of the Montessori philosophy of education. Maria Montessori believed that her method of education produced a new kind of human being, conscious of his unity with all other human beings, past and present, everywhere on the globe.

"Preventing conflicts is the work of politics; establishing peace is the work of education," she said in a speech before the European Congress for Peace in Brussels in 1936, just before the outbreak of World War II.[1] And, in a speech in Copenhagen in 1937, she states that, "Education is the best weapon for peace."[2]

The concept of peace is something that is valued and taught in our Montessori classrooms. Children learn to sing songs about peace, like "Building Bridges," and they do art projects to express their ideas of what peace means.

Many Montessori schools have a "peace pole" near the entrance of the buildings with the word *peace* on it in various languages. Schools celebrate special days to focus on world peace. When conflicts break out somewhere across the globe, we often lead discussions about peaceful ways to resolve world conflicts.

[1]Montessori, Maria, *Education and Peace* (Oxford, England: Clio Press, 1995), 24.
[2]Ibid, 28.

An important element in the prepared environment is a "peace table" somewhere in the classroom. This might be complemented with representations of the four elements —a wind chime for *air*, a small vase of *water*, a candle lit at ceremonial times for *fire*, and a bowl of dirt for *earth*.

Such a peace table offers a place for students to go to calm themselves when they are feeling stressed, a place for two students to go to resolve a disagreement, or a center of focus for a class meditation or centering exercise. Its very presence proclaims to the students that this classroom is intended to be a place of peace.

On a deeper level, one of the principal tools for building a sense of peace is the Cosmic Education curriculum, the multi-chapter origin story exploring where we come from as a species. As students learn their origins, they become more conscious and aware of the essential unity of the human race, the fact that we are a single species, belonging to the same family.[3]

This heightened sense of human community can contribute to the self-discipline we seek in our students.

• Conflict Resolution Skills

Even with the most careful preparation of the environment and community building, there are inevitable conflicts that arise among students. In fact, there is more opportunity for this in Montessori classrooms than in traditional classes.

If you sit all day at a desk, silent and forbidden to interact with your peers, there is little opportunity for conflict until you get outside the classroom at recess or lunch period. But in a Montessori classroom, children are inter-acting with each other all day long, and they are going to have their share of disagreements.

Students have to be taught, under our guidance and leadership, how to resolve their conflicts peacefully. Children in lower

---

[3] Duffy, Michael and D'Neil, *Children of the Universe: Cosmic Education in the Montessori Elementary Classroom* (Hollidaysburg, PA: Parent Child Press, 2002), 128-131.

elementary can be taught to use "I messages" to express their feelings of anger, frustration, or fear. They can be taught how to look for "win-win" solutions to disagreements. And, at the upper elementary level, they can even be introduced to formal devices such as peer mediation to help resolve simmering conflicts.

In the long run, taking class time to teach these skills does not detract from academics. It is an investment that pays incalculable dividends with children at an age when relations with peers weigh so heavily on their emotional life. It builds community and provides the basis for self-discipline.

• **Centering Activities**

Many of our Montessori elementary classrooms begin the school day with some type of centering activity.

This is a logical extension of Montessori's use of the "silence game" with primary students, where children sit as quietly as they possibly can for several minutes at a time. It is a way of practicing *collective obedience* or whole group self-discipline.

At the elementary level, this takes the form of a quiet time for students to focus as a preparation for immersion in work. Some schools call this a "meditation," with the teacher or one of the older students leading the children in a guided visualization of some calm and pleasant scene. Others, in an attempt to avoid any overtones of religion, call it a "centering" activity, where children are invited to sit quietly, find their center in an almost physical way, practice deep breathing on a conscious level, and/or spend some time in reflection.

Still other schools use Yoga exercises geared to children, including stretching and poses. Brain Gym is another technique, consisting in a series of movements and activities that help children cross the midline and integrate the portions of their brain (a practice also called Educational Kinesiology,[4] developed by Paul and Gail Dennison).

[4]See www.braingym.org for further information.

Whichever approach we chose, all these activities are designed to calm the inner spirit of the children and help them focus in preparation for the work of the day. It doesn't take long—5 to 10 minutes at most—but it has the effect of preparing the students for several hours of maximum concentration and self-discipline.

• Class Meetings

We highly recommend instituting a system of class meetings to discuss issues that affect the whole class. This is particularly appropriate for an age where the infusion of *democracy* into the classroom context is more and more validated by research.

With this technique, students—or the teacher—raise an issue by listing it on a clipboard or white board accessible to the whole class. For example, "I am bothered by the fact that I never find materials in good order when I take them off the shelves."

At a class assembly or circle time, the person who raised the issue—it must be signed!—explains the problem, and the group then decides whether it is an issue that affects the whole class or just one student. If it affects the class as a whole, it becomes the subject of a class meeting.

Roles are assigned—discussion leader (not necessarily the teacher), a recorder (who writes down ideas on a poster or dry erase board), a timekeeper (who keeps track of agreed upon limits for the discussion), and a task master (who reminds students when they ignore the rules of discussion). The recorder then writes down the problem and a discussion of "solutions" begins.

This is a time for sitting in a circle and brainstorming ways to solve the problem. Each person in the community is given a chance to contribute by offering a solution, agreeing with a previous suggestion by saying "ditto," or by passing. No ideas are considered unacceptable, and there is no discussion allowed at this time.

Going around the circle at least twice gives everyone an opportunity to offer solutions. Discussion follows on the meaning and/or the merits of each suggestion. Then a sub-group is assigned to align similar solutions and to return to a later session with a newly ordered list of suggestions.

At this later session, everyone again has a chance to speak, in hopes that a consensus will emerge. When the list is winnowed down to two or three popular suggestions, a vote is taken to decide which solution to adopt. Before it is formally accepted, each person in the community must feel that the suggestion with the most votes represents a strategy worth trying.

We have found that this is an invaluable technique for dealing with problems as they arise and for practicing genuine democracy in the classroom setting. Students feel empowered and invested in the solution because it is their work rather than a decree from us—leading to the self-discipline envisioned by Montessori.

• Montessori Speak

There is a language that we use as Montessori teachers that attempts to focus on the positive rather than the negative in dealing with our students, ways to guide children with respect and encourage self-discipline.

Language is important, and we generally try to avoid blaming, belittling, intimidation, commands, lecturing, nagging, name-calling, sarcasm, comparisons and, of course, physical punishment. None of these techniques have a place in a Montessori classroom. Experts on parenting and child psychologists have all come to recognize that such methods produce only short-term results, and we are trained to avoid such techniques.

Some of the language we typically use in a Montessori class-room include: "You have a choice...", to put the responsibility for decisions back on the student; "I'm sorry you have chosen to...", when students make bad choices; "That behavior is inappropriate in our class," to address willful misbehavior or or disrespect of others; "I'm waiting for everyone to get ready so we can start the lesson," to ask for respect of the group and invite the children to regulate their own behavior.

As Montessori teachers, we need to be soft in the center and firm around the edges, always approaching children with gentleness and quiet calmness when we feel the need to intervene to remind them of the limits on their freedom to be respectful of the community.

All of the strategies listed above can be used in classrooms to create the kind of "self-disciplined" classroom community that Montessori advocated.

Leadership Strategies to Support Student Autonomy

There are other tactics we can employ to encourage the autonomy and auto-education that serve as the basis for intrinsic motivation.

Obviously, we can talk to children about assuming responsibility for their own learning, but actions on our part are far more effective. The way we go about content delivery, evaluation and setting expectations can either hinder or foster our students' responsibility for their own learning.

• Answering Questions

We should avoid answering children's questions too readily. That seems counter-intuitive to our usual understanding of the role of teachers in a classroom, but it is important to undergo a transformation in the way we think about our role in dispensing information.

When a student gets in the habit of going to us for answers, this produces a dependence that goes contrary to the goals of self-direction and auto-education. When students ask questions, the response might be, "I wonder where you could find the answer to that question. How about doing some research and letting me and the rest of the class know what you find?"

We have to get away from the idea that we are the source of all information in the class—a role which teachers (and textbooks) play in traditional classrooms. That leaves nothing for students to find out on their own and implies that what we tell them is all there is to know about the subject. As long as we answer students' questions, showing off our store of knowledge, we deprive them of the opportunity to discover information for themselves.

In our school, we had a "three before me" rule. We asked students, before they came to us for help, to first take three steps: 1) ask yourself if you can think of the answer or a way to locate the answer; 2) ask a friend to help you find the answer; 3) ask an older or more knowledgeable student for help. If you have done all three steps without finding a satisfactory answer to your question, only then should you approach one of the adults (teacher or assistant).

Then, if we are fulfilling our role correctly, the more appropriate answer is usually, "Let me help point you in the direction of where you night find that answer" or "Let's look together for information that might help us find that answer" instead of simply supplying the answer.

• Content Control

Closely related to the previous suggestion is one about content control. We should avoid telling students everything we know about a subject in our lessons. It's always tempting to show off our knowledge when we are giving a lesson, whether it's describing the classification of animals or telling them about the causes of the American Revolution.

Lessons are intended to be impressionistic, overviews of a subject, with the goal of giving students a context for understanding and seducing them into wanting to learn more on their own. This means that there is no place for a 45-minute lecture on any subject. Lessons are short and to the point, with most of the exploration of the subject left to the students. Only in this way do we avoid limiting the scope of their knowledge (ala textbook learning) and give them room to auto-educate, exploring a subject as far as their interest takes them.

This doesn't mean that we don't need to know our subject matter. It is only with a thorough knowledge of the formation of the early universe, the emergence of our solar system, the geological formation of our planet, the evolution of life on that planet, and the history of our human species and human societies, that we can give the proper context and be passionate enough to lure our students into wanting to know more themselves.

• **Checking Work vs. Self-Correction**

One of the principal roles of teachers in traditional schools is to check student work, correcting mistakes and assigning grades. Montessori believes more in self-correction.

She designed many of her materials with this in mind. For example, classified nomenclature materials in lower elementary in Biology, Geography and History have their own control booklets, so students can check their own work rather than waiting for us to see if they matched pictures, labels and definitions correctly.

Or consider a student doing a division problem with a multi-digit divisor with the test tube division materials. He knows that, as he distributes the beads and records his work, when the number he gets after he performs the subtraction step doesn't correspond to the number of beads left in the bowls, he has made a mistake.

We should make every effort to give students tools to discover their own mistakes rather than having to turn in their work to be checked and getting it back with red marks in their notebooks.

There are important psychological differences between adult corrections and self-correction. Adult corrections tend to create discouraged learners who feel like they never get things right; self-correction leads to feelings of pride at having figured something out on their own and it promotes meta-cognition (knowing what we know), one of the highest forms of knowledge.

Requiring students to have their work checked by us or our assistant sends them the message that their work "doesn't count" or have any proven validity until it is checked off by an adult. Giving them tools to check their own work leaves them in control of their own learning and self-evaluation, a much less threatening situation for eventual motivation to do more work.

This doesn't mean that we abdicate our accountability for monitoring student work. Our main tool for this is observation of the students as they work, with occasional spot checks of recorded work.

• Mini-Conferences

One other way to monitor student work without interfering with their autonomy is the mini-conference. Every week or two, we can sit down with students one at a time to review their work since the last mini-conference.

The student brings his notebooks and work journal, and we and the student go over the work to evaluate his performance. The primary responsibility for evaluation should remain with the student (building meta-cognition), but we can make note of areas where he might be struggling with basic skills and address them in future lessons.

This can seem like a very labor-intensive, time-consuming practice, but these sessions can be brief, lasting no more than 10-15 minutes. Once students know the routine, they will show up prepared, with all of their work and some idea of how to present it to us. We may also discover over time that some students are very dependable, and may need a mini-conference only every two weeks or even every month; others may need to be checked every week to make sure they are not taking short cuts or paying little attention to the quality of their work.

If done in this way, mini-conferences are likely to take up no more than a full morning or afternoon, perhaps on a Friday to evaluate the preceding week and set goals for the following week. It can also be a time to select work to include in the student's portfolio.

• Portfolios

Portfolios consist in a collection of representative work, chosen over time, to document student progress in the various subject areas of the curriculum. They are a tool much more appropriate for evaluation of Montessori students than standardized tests or grades.

Students should be allowed to choose, with some guidance from us, samples of work to include in the portfolio, making sure that each item has their name and a date on it. Their choices should represent work that they are particularly proud of, work that is representative of their best efforts in different subject areas.

This collection of work provides documentation of student progress in the various subject areas, allowing us to compare work from months ago or even previous years to see what progress has been made. This can be the raw material for preparing parent conferences, for spotting problem areas where sufficient progress is not being made, and for evaluating student progress when grades or other evaluation systems need to be applied.

Perhaps most importantly, it allows students to monitor their own work, giving them one more tool for owning their own learning.

• Follow Up Work

Students should always be expected to do something after a lesson, preferably with materials—not just memorize and regurgitate what we presented them in the lesson. This is what we refer to as *follow up work.*

The principal reason we insist on follow up work is that this is the second period of learning in a three-period learning format. The first period is the teacher's gift of a presentation; the second period is the time for student practice of a skill or pursuit of further information; the third period consists in the student-teacher evaluation of how well the subject has been learned.

All too often, we may be tempted to jump from first period to third without allowing students time for second period work, as though all it takes is a well delivered lesson for students to learn something. But Montessori believed that real learning takes place when students are active in their pursuit of knowledge, manipulating the materials to discover something new or expanding their knowledge through research. This is when auto-education takes place.

Montessori said it was engagement with a material or work that allows a child to become normalized or self-disciplined; it is also this engagement that promotes auto-education and intrinsic motivation, giving students ownership of the learning process.

That means we ourselves must be convinced of the value of the materials. Young children are perceptive. They can read our actions and our attitudes much better than they can adhere to our words. If our students are reluctant to use the materials, the first question we should ask ourselves is whether *we* are really convinced of their value.

Another part of our responsibility is to be a good *technician*, able to show students how to use the materials and deliver a good lesson. For lessons to go well, we need to fully understand how to use the materials involved and to manipulate them without stumbling. In some cases this can take a fair amount of practice.

Finally, we need to insist that our students use materials after every lesson. We have learned over years of teaching adults in Montessori training courses that no matter how expertly we model a presentation, the student teachers generally don't know how to use the materials until they get their hands on them, often ending a session with the exclamation, "Oh, now I get it!" Our children are no different.

• Work Plans vs. Work Journals

Most of our classrooms have some system of letting children know what work is expected of them—a list of choices on a board posted in the room, a written work plan for each student every week, or simply verbal instructions before sending children to work each day. While this kind of guidance is necessary at the beginning of a school year, the ideal is to transfer responsibility for this choosing to the students.

All too often we hear students with specific work plans saying, "I'm finished with my work," and proceeding to play around the rest of the day. Giving students a work plan with everything filled in by us creates a *check off* mentality that promotes getting work done quickly so children can be free to just socialize and play.

The goal for Montessori, by contrast, is to have students become engaged in work in a concentrated way that allows them to practice self-discipline and maximizes the internal development that comes from auto-education. Lists don't lend themselves to this kind of work.

Obviously, some element of teacher dictation of tasks is necessary for students new to Montessori, for those entering a new level, and for almost all students at the beginning of a school year. But we can wean them from dependence on these lists as soon as they are able to choose on their own. Then work plans can be turned into *work journals*, where students record the work they have done rather than check off the work assigned by us.

An important point to make here is that we don't need to use the same system for every student in the class, or even for every child at each grade level. Students who are capable of taking responsibility for their own work should not be penalized and denied the opportunity to exercise that responsibility simply because there are some children who cannot handle it without more intensive hand holding.

Once again, the bottom line is to encourage student ownership of learning in every way we can, rather than unwittingly to stand in the way.

Conclusion

These are some of the strategies that can be used in our classrooms to promote self-discipline and auto-education. Everything we do to support student ownership of their behavior and their learning helps them to become intrinsically motivated.

But this doesn't seem to be enough for all of our students. Despite our best efforts to engage them in work, the way Montessori envisioned, some of them manage to remain in a distracted state of constant wandering and need for re-direction to their work.

Are there techniques that modern science has discovered that can complement what we know from our training and enhance student motivation? Can we reach those wandering students and get even our best students more highly motivated?

That's the focus of the remaining chapters of Part 2.

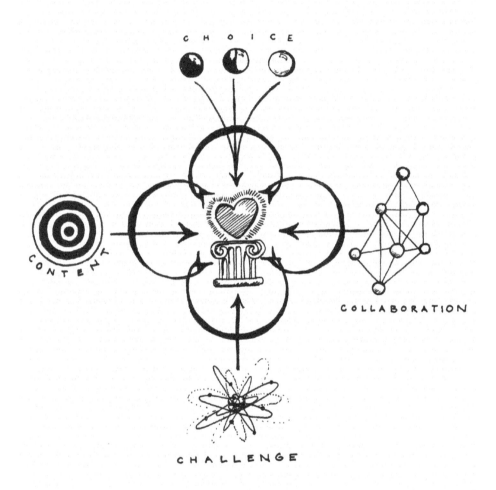

CHOICE

CONTENT

COLLABORATION

CHALLENGE

Chapter 6

The Four Cs: The Science of Intrinsic Motivation

Let's assume that we firmly believe in the principles outlined in Part 1 and try not to sabotage those principles with our students, and that we are using most of the practices we suggested in the last chapter.

We've used every strategy in the Montessori playbook to make sure our students are motivated and engaged in learning.

It seems to be working for the majority of our class. But there are still days when even our best students don't seem motivated. And there are some who appear to be perpetually distracted, resistant to using the materials or doing any focused work that we would expect for their academic advancement.

These latter students frequently disrupt the calm of the class, they are defiant toward any attempts to get them to work, and they take up an enormous amount of our time and energy in trying to keep them occupied in any productive activity in the class.

How do we reach these unmotivated students?

The formula that decades of scientific research suggest is that there are four important elements in promoting intrinsic motivation—choice, content, collaboration, and challenge.

All of these elements are already part of our Montessori classrooms in one way or another. However, there are some important related insights to be gained from modern science.

First, we have not always thought of these four elements as means to intrinsic motivation for our students. We include them in our classrooms for a variety of important reasons, but we may not be aware of how important they are specifically for intrinsic motivation.

Second, these are the four elements that have been identified by decades of scientific research into intrinsic motivation. We may have an intuitive grasp of the value of these strategies, but we now have proven research to back them up and we need to examine the practical implications of that body of research.

Finally, it is only by isolating these classroom practices that we can examine whether we are making the best and most efficient use of them to promote and support intrinsic motivation. That's going to be the focus of the next four chapters.

So, how did we decide on these four elements, and how do we know they are so important to intrinsic motivation?

The first point to make here is a caution that we have to be careful about self-professed experts on motivation to make sure their goal is not to get our students to simply do our bidding. That's not motivation—that's manipulation!

As adults, we have a bag full of tricks that we could use to get students to do what we want them to do, at least in the short term. But, given Montessori's clear advocacy for intrinsic motivation, that is not the goal of Montessori education. That really amounts to nothing more than manipulation of smaller bodies to do what the larger, supposedly wiser bodies in the room want them to do.

"'How do I get kids motivated?' is a question that not only misreads the nature of motivation but also operates within a paradigm of control, the very thing that is death to motivation," writes Kohn. "...the job of educators is neither to make students motivated nor to sit passively; it is to set up the conditions that make learning possible."[1]

What are those conditions? Or to put it in Montessori jargon, what are the elements in the prepared environment to promote real, intrinsic motivation in our students?

This is where we seek the guidance of experts who have studied modern research on intrinsic motivation for clues on how to reach all of our students more effectively and, particularly, those seemingly unmotivated ones. We need to make sure the *experts* we are using are trying to achieve the same goals as Montessori.

---

[1] Kohn, *Punished,* 199.

Kohn is one expert who believes in the same principles of self-control, self-directed learning and intrinsic motivation as Montessori did. Another is Pink, whom we also met in earlier chapters. Because neither of these authors is coming from a potentially biased Montessori viewpoint, they will be our main authorities for our list of four C's.

Both of these authors have extensively examined the educational literature and research behind intrinsic motivation. From that examination, they have produced formulas for motivating students that are less about manipulating them to do an adult's bidding than providing them with a learning environment in which they can operate with intrinsic motivation.

It is no accident that both of these authors were keynote speakers at national conferences of the American Montessori Society (AMS) in recent years. Organizers of those conferences recognized that these men had something important to offer to the Montessori community.

Their goals are the same as those of Montessori, but they are more systematic in their analysis of what is involved, and their suggestions are based on much more scientific research than the anecdotal observations of Montessori. So, there is much that we can learn from them.

Two other experts we drew from for our list are Angela Murray, research coordinator for AMS and author of a 2011 *Montessori Life*[2] article on motivation; and Angeline Stoll Lillard, author of *Montessori: The Science Behind the Genius.*[3]

Murray brings together recent research on motivation, using her own sources—Edward Deci and Richard Ryan (who were also sources for Kohn and Pink), T.L. Seifert (2004),[4] and P.R. Pintrich (2003).[5]

Lillard's book, while not directly devoted to the topic of motivation, is based on a wealth of research studies that support Montessori principles, including elements of motivation.

---

[2]Murray, Angela, "Montessori Elementary Philosophy Reflects Current Motivation Theories," *Montessori Life, Vol. 23, No. 1 (Spring 2011),* 22-33.

[3]Lillard, Angeline Stoll, *Montessori: The Science Behind the Genius* (New York: Oxford University Press, 2005).

[4]Seifert, T.L.,"Understanding Student Motivation," *Educational Research* (2004) 46: 136-149.

[5]Pintrich, P.R., "A Motivational Science Perspective on the Role of Student Motivation in Learning and Teaching Contexts," *Journal of Educational Psychology* (2003) 95: 667-686.

We will find that their Montessori perspective coincides with that of outside experts like Kohn and Pink.

Let's see what all of these experts have to say about the four C's of motivation that we have identified.

• Choice

The first element that all of these experts agree on is that of *choice*. All of them contend that choice is an essential element in promoting intrinsic motivation.

In arguing for *choice* in the classroom, Kohn says, "deprive children of self-determination and you deprive them of motivation...Every day ought to include at least one block of time in which children can decide what to do."[6]

We Montessori teachers will recognize this as what we refer to as "uninterrupted work time." There's not just one block of time in which children decide what to do; individual choice fills the majority of the child's day in our classrooms.

Pink, for his part, calls this element by the terminology of *autonomy*, and states that it is different than pure independence. "It's not the rugged, go-it-alone, rely-on-nobody individualism of the American cowboy. It means acting with choice – which means we can be both autonomous and happily interdependent with others."[7]

That sounds very much like our Montessori version of independence and interdependence at the same time. What's important here is that Pink calls autonomy *acting with choice*, similar to the element of choice cited by Kohn.

It should be noted that when we discussed autonomy in Part 1, we were speaking primarily of Montessori's notion of autonomous learning or auto-education. Kohn and Drive do not address this as directly, and their focus is on the related but distinct notion of choice.

[6]Kohn, *Punished*, 221-223.
[7]Pink, *Drive*, 90.

Choice and autonomy are certainly closely related. Choice feeds autonomy, and autonomy usually requires choice. But you can, in theory, have auto-education without choice and vice versa, so we will examine choice as an element distinct from auto-education.

Murray, for her part, also uses the terminology of *autonomy* as one of the elements of intrinsic motivation. While including a discussion of some of the things we spoke about in the chapter on autonomous learning, she makes clear that choice is at the root of student motivation.

Lillard, who dedicated a whole chapter of her book to the element of choice, concludes from the research she examined, that "both in adults and children, the provision of choice is associated with several positive consequences. People learn and remember better, solve tasks better, and opt to engage in tasks more and longer when they think they have more control."[8]

The positive consequences that Lillard cites are the touchstones that researchers look for in determining whether a strategy is effective or not, whether it produces real and lasting motivation or not.

• Content

All of our experts also agree on the important place that *content* plays in intrinsic motivation. What we teach and what we ask our students to learn has a major impact on whether they are motivated.

In dealing with *content*, Kohn argues that content must be meaningful or as he puts it, "things worth knowing."

"The premise of the entire discussion is that children are people who have lives and interests outside of school, who walk into the classroom with their own perspectives, points of view, ways of making sense of things and

---

[8]Lillard, *Science*, 86.

formulating meaning," he writes. "What we teach and how we teach must take account of those realities."[9]

This is what we in Montessori refer to as "following the child," with a curriculum and pedagogical approach that is highly individualized for each student in our class.

Once again, Pink uses different terminology—*purpose*—that both includes the element of content and goes somewhat beyond what Kohn is describing. "The most deeply motivated people—not to mention those who are most productive and satisfied—hitch their desires to a cause larger than themselves,"[10] Pink writes, primarily in the context of subjects older than school-age children.

Montessori education, however, certainly strives to lure elementary aged students into something larger than themselves, particularly through the Cosmic Education curriculum.

Murray describes this element as *interest/meaning*, noting, "Maria Montessori believed that interest is an important companion to self-determination in fostering internalized student motivation."[11]

Lillard devotes an entire chapter of her book to the topic of *interest*. She begins by declaring, "Montessori education is designed to awaken interest and to allow children to pursue learning about issues that already personally interest them. This is a natural corollary to a system of education based on choice: one chooses to do what one is interested in doing. It is also necessary to a system that is based on intrinsic motivation."[12]

---

[9] Kohn, *Punished*, 219.
[10] Pink, *Drive*, 133.
[11] Murray, "Philosophy Reflects," 27.
[12] Lillard, *Science*, 114.

• Collaboration

Collaboration is another factor in intrinsic motivation cited by Kohn. Pink does not mention this element, but Murray and Lillard both link collaboration to intrinsic motivation.

Kohn writes, "As thinkers such as Piaget and Dewey have explained, learning at its best is the result of sharing information and ideas, challenging someone else's interpretation and having to rethink your own, working on problems in a climate of social support." Later he adds, "The opportunity to *collaborate* ought to be the default condition in the classroom—the arrangement that is used most of the day, except when there is good reason to do things another way."[13]

That is certainly not a practice that is foreign to us as Montessori teachers. Collaboration is the dominant mode of activity in our elementary classrooms.

Murray refers to this element as *relatedness*, crediting Ryan and Deci (2000)[14] for articulating the need to feel connected with others as important for intrinsic motivation. "Montessori education clearly leverages the power of elementary children's social tendencies as a means of fostering motivation,"[15] Murray writes.

Lillard, in concluding a chapter in her book on *learning from peers*, argues that collaboration "probably motivates learning, as suggested by the studies showing high levels of student satisfaction with peer learning situations."[16]

In the view of all three of these experts, collaboration enhances intrinsic motivation.

---

[13]Kohn, *Punished*, 214-215.
[14]Ryan, R.M. and E.L. Deci, "Self-determination theory and the facilitation of intrinsic motivation, social development, and well-being," *American Psychologist* (2000), 55: 68-78.
[15]Murray, "Philosophy Reflects," 31.
[16]Lillard, *Science*, 222.

• **Challenge**

Pink refers to this element as *mastery*, Kohn does not include it in his list, Murray calls it *competence*, while Lillard addresses the issue of *mastery* and motivation in the course of her discussion about interest.

Pink defines *mastery* as "the desire to get better and better at something that matters."[17] And he argues that activities must be chosen to avoid giving people a feeling of being "overwhelmed or underwhelmed with their work."[18]

We will see that this relates to our job of finding a happy balance between challenge and success for our students. This is something that we teachers struggle to achieve every day with every student.

Murray, in discussing *competence*, concludes that the research she examined links this element with all the other elements, and she says, "competence establishes expectations of future success. This expectation motivates effort directed toward meeting new challenges...competence begets confidence, which in turn inspires children to tackle subsequent challenges."[19]

Lillard, in comparing people who are driven by the desire for *mastery* rather than performance goals, says the research shows that "People with mastery orientations, in brief, are people who are interested in learning in order to master a topic. They tend to like challenges, and they persist in them. People with performance goals, in contrast, tend to like to do easy jobs that make them look good."[20]

We prefer to call the final element *challenge* rather than mastery or competence because, we believe, it more clearly evokes the place of this element in motivation. As we will see,

[17]Pink, *Drive,* 111.
[18]Ibid, 117.
[19]Murray, "Philosophy Reflects," 28.
[20]Lillard, *Science,* 149.

it involves finding just the right level of difficulty for our students in their work, requiring effort on their part but setting them up for success rather than failure.

Conclusion

These four C's—choice, content, collaboration, challenge—provide us with a framework for a prepared environment that the science of researchers tells us will promote intrinsic motivation as envisioned by Montessori as well as the modern authors whom we cite above. By paying special attention to these elements in the prepared environment, perhaps we can reach those unmotivated students who have so far failed to respond to all our strategies.

There are no magic formulas that will reach every single student in our class, and our implementation of these ideas will nearly always be less than perfect. Our hope is that attention to the four C's will provide additional opportunities for those unmotivated students to finally engage in productive work with joy and passion.

In the following chapters we will discuss these elements one at a time to determine how we can best implement them to support and promote love of learning.

Chapter 7

Choice: Empowering Student Motivation

Choice is identified by all of the experts as one of the keys to intrinsic motivation. In a Montessori context, choice is already an essential requirement for the development of self-discipline and auto-education. Without choice, students cannot develop any self-directed sense of responsibility or take charge of their own learning.

In addition, we can say that without choice, they will be doomed to dependence on the external motivators of reward and punishment and unable to develop intrinsic motivation.

Kohn's rationale for giving students choice in their work is threefold:

1) it is a more respectful way of dealing with others;

2) it makes teaching more enjoyable as a shared enterprise with the students; and

3) it simply "works better," producing better results in the long run.[1]

The last reason is the most important, and Kohn cites numerous studies, at all age levels, to demonstrate the effectiveness of choice. Here is a sampling of those applying to elementary aged students:

- Second graders in Pittsburgh, given choice in which tasks they would work on in a given time, tended to "complete more learning tasks in less time,"[2] a pretty good indicator of motivation.

---

[1]Kohn, *Punished*, 221-222.
[2]Wang, Margaret C., and Billie Stiles, "An investigation of Children's Concept of Self-Responsibility for Their School Learning," *American Educational Research Journal* [13] (1976): 159-179.

- Teachers of inner-city children trained to promote self-determination produced students who missed less school and scored better on tests of basic skills than those in conventional classrooms.[3]

- Fourth- fifth- and sixth-graders given personal responsibility for their studies had "significantly higher self-esteem and perceived academic competence" than children in controlled classrooms.[4]

Pink, in arguing for autonomy and choice, begins with the premise that "our basic nature is to be curious and self-directed...Have you ever seen a six-month-old or a one-year-old who's *not* curious and self-directed. I haven't. That's how we are out of the box. If, at age fourteen or forty-three, we're passive and inert, that's not because it's our nature. It's because something flipped our default setting."[5]

Pink maintains that a gradual loss of autonomy is responsible for dampening that natural curiosity of the young child, and that choice provides the child with the opportunity to become both autonomous and interdependent with others.

"According to a cluster of recent behavioral science studies," he writes, "autonomous motivation promotes greater conceptual understanding, better grades, enhanced persistence at school and in sporting activities, higher productivity, less burnout, and greater levels of psychological well-being."[6]

Pink advocates for choice in four areas: what people do, when they do it, how they do it, and whom they do it with. While cautioning that autonomy doesn't mean an abandonment of accountability, he describes numerous experiments in the world of business that indicate that choice in these four areas—task, time, technique, and team—have a great impact on the successful outcome of work tasks.

---

[3]deCharms, Richard, "Personal Causation Training in Schools," *Journal of Applied Social Psychology* 2 (1972): 95-113.
[4]Ryan, Richard M. and Wendy S. Grolnick. "Origins and Pawns in the Classroom: Self-Report and Projective Assessments of Individual Differences in Children's Perceptions," *Journal of Personality and Social Psychology* 50 (1986): 550-58.
[5]Pink, *Drive*, 89.
[6]Ibid, 90-91.

These four aspects of choice should also be a litmus test for the way we run our Montessori classrooms. Students should have real choice in the work they do, in what part of the day or week they decide to do it, in the approach they take to the work, and in their selection of working companions. None of these areas of choice is absolute, but each is important in its own way and should be maximized as much as possible. Imposing limits in any of these areas necessarily reduces the intrinsic motivation of the students.

Lillard has gathered her own collection of research literature to back the importance of choice, summing it up by saying, "both in adults and children, the provision of choice is associated with several positive consequences. People learn and remember better, solve tasks better, and opt to engage in tasks more and longer when they think they have more control."[7]

The criteria Lillard mentions—better recall, problem-solving and opting to engage in tasks longer and more frequently—are the criteria researchers use to determine whether a specific technique is effective or not. She cites studies to show that choice is an important motivating factor to achieve these outcomes.

- In one study, first- to third-graders were presented a drawing activity as either a choice or an assignment. Those in the choice group drew for an average of five minutes, compared to just a minute and a half for the assignment group.[8]

- In another study, 7- to 9-year-olds were asked to solve anagrams, with one group being given the chance to choose the categories of subjects (e.g. animals, food, etc.), another group was told their mothers had chosen for them, and a third group was told the experimenter had chosen. Even though the puzzles were yoked and all three groups were given the same anagrams as chosen by the first group, the free choice group solved twice as many anagrams as either of the other two groups.[9]

---

[7]Lillard, *Science*, 86.

[8]Ibid, 84. Citing W.B. Swann & T.S. Pittman, (1977). "Initiating play activity of children: The moderating influence of verbal cues on intrinsic motivation," *Child Development* 48 (3), 1128-32.

[9]Lillard, p. 83. Citing S.S. Iyenger & M.R. Lepper, (2000). "When choice is demotivating: Can one desire too much of a good thing?" *Journal of Personality & Social Psychology* 79(6), 995-1006.

Those of us in Montessori might be feeling a little smug at this point, thinking that our students are given wide discretion about things that matter in the classroom such as where they sit, whom they work with, and when they do their math problems. Instead of just one block of free time each day, as advocated by Kohn, their entire day is virtually a continuous block of free time for them to work independently.

But that's only true if we are giving them genuine choices. It's only if we have actually been converted to the Montessori philosophy and given up our need for control.

Let's examine some practical areas to make sure we are giving our students the maximum amount of choices they need to keep them motivated – especially those we complain about as being unmotivated. We'll use Pink's list of the four T's to examine our practice.

Task

To what extent do our students really have choice in their work tasks?

If, as lower elementary teachers, we tell our students that we expect all of them to make a wall chart after a lesson on the external parts of the fish, there's a good chance at least one child might not want to make a wall chart. Perhaps he would prefer to make a freehand drawing of a fish in his notebook and label it himself, a poster-sized fish with parts identified in a web-like array of labels, or a clay model of the various fish parts.

If, as upper elementary teachers, we expect all of our students to do the same research or identical follow up work after a lesson on causes of the American Revolution, what are the chances that *all* of them are going to be interested? That *unmotivated* student might simply prefer to study the causes of the revolution through its principal characters. The outcome of knowledge would be about the same, with the added interest of a survey of the most important American patriots.

One obvious way for us to make choice available to our students is that we should always have several options for follow up work after each lesson. In a study of the 13 original American colonies, if a student chooses a colony that became the state where his grandmother grew up instead of all 13 or one assigned by us, he is more likely to be interested in doing the research.

Furthermore, what's wrong with giving our students a chance to design their *own* follow up work after a lesson? You might be surprised at their creativity and the level of challenge they create for themselves when given a real choice.

Could this actually work? Giving upper elementary students a choice of whether they want to research the geography, political life, religion, housing, or daily life of ancient Egypt, allows them to decide which element of the lesson they want to pursue. Lower elementary students can be allowed to pick out the creatures on the Timeline of Life that they want to learn more about.

This might be acceptable for the cultural subjects, but what about Math, Geometry, and Language? If we give a lesson on dynamic addition with the stamp game, is there really any choice possible in the follow up work? Yes, there is.

For one thing, students don't have to work off those store-bought problem sets that take the burden off us to make up our own problems. Why not let *students* make up their own problems (with some guidance about not using big numbers in the thousands digit that would go beyond the inherent limitations of the materials)?

There is a major psychological difference between doing problem card A43 and choosing your own numbers to calculate—and that could mean the difference for that unmotivated child. A43 might work great for three of the four children at the lesson, but it might be a stumbling block for that fourth child.

Another possible area of choice is the number of problems we expect students to do with the materials before the next lesson. If everyone is expected to do the same number of problems, that seems fair to everybody and less of a hassle for record-keeping. But not every student will need the same number of problems to master the process of dynamic addition.

Why not ask students how many problems they think they need to do to master dynamic addition—fostering metacognition—and let them choose their own number of problems? One student might choose one problem per day, another might say he will practice it three times in one sitting, another will say he doesn't need to do any problems. That last choice is not an acceptable option, since we should expect every child to do at least one problem with the materials to experience second period learning.

So, our unmotivated student chooses—reluctantly—to do only one problem. What's the consequence? When we do a quick review at the beginning of the next lesson, it should be clear that some choices don't work and have to be reconsidered. If the student discovers for himself that one problem is not enough to "get it," he will be more likely to willingly choose three or four problems at his next opportunity.

Choice is a motivator. It gives any student a sense of control, leads to more interest in the work, and produces better results in the long run. Children are people, just like us, and choice is important to both of us.

"Every teacher who is told what material to cover, when to cover it, and how to evaluate children's performance is a teacher who knows that enthusiasm for one's work quickly evaporates in the face of control," writes Kohn. "Not every teacher realizes, however, that exactly the same is true of students: deprive children of self-determination and you deprive them of motivation."[10]

Time

Time is another area we need to examine in our practice, as to when we expect our students to do their work.

If we tell our students that the morning work period is for math and language, and the cultural curriculum can only be worked on in the afternoons, we have deprived them of an important element of choice. Maybe a child likes to start his day with some exciting cultural work and plans to get to his math later in the day.

If we set up our class so that Tuesdays are geometry days, and students are expected to work on geometry that day of the week, we have taken away an opportunity for them to develop their own abilities for time management.

---

[10]Kohn, *Punished*, 221.

It's probably also a mistake for us to put time limits on student work. While it is reasonable to have some kind of deadlines for completion of work, we should not be too anxious to move our students along so we can go on to the next lesson. As long as our students *choose* to be genuinely engaged in some piece of work, we should not cut short their effort before it is exhausted. This imposes an artificial time limit on how far they can go in a subject.

Whenever possible, students should be free to choose the time to do their work. If we instead impose time frames on them, intrinsic motivation could be reduced proportionately.

It is particularly disturbing to us to visit Montessori elementary classrooms where there is a rule that daily math and language work must be completed before students are allowed to work in the cultural area. That can kill the enthusiasm and engagement that can come from *any* type of work. Montessori believed that a high level of focus, more than proficiency in math and language, is needed to normalize children and lead to real enthusiasm for learning.

If a child is more attracted to animals than to numbers, we could let him get engaged with the First Knowledge of Animals when he starts his school day. That enthusiasm and focus might just carry over to his doing a bead frame subtraction problem later in the day. If we make him do the bead frame problem first, he may spend the entire day putting it off and getting nothing done.

Another reason we are disturbed by the "math-language first" rule is that it gives students the message that these are the really important subjects and the cultural subjects are like dessert that you get to enjoy if you eat your vegetables first. That's a subtle surrender to society's insane emphasis on standardized testing (generally confined to math and language), a denigration of the joy that can come from math and language, and a denial of the supremacy that Montessori placed on the cultural curriculum under the rubric of Cosmic Education.

Technique

Do we provide students with choice in the way they do their work?

When we want a child to work on addition memorization, do we expect him to move lock-step through the sequence of strip board, finger number one, finger board number two, finger board number three, bingo board, snake game? Or is the choice of material up to him when he wants to practice his addition facts?

A certain type of child may be totally frustrated by the requirement of laying out the blue and red strips in a neat half pyramid alongside the strip board, but have no problem with moving his fingers to find the answer on the first finger board. To insist that he first practice with the strip board can easily create one of those *unmotivated* students we worry so much about.

In upper elementary, are written research reports the only acceptable way to do follow up work? A student who makes a scale model of the Acropolis will probably learn as much about important facets of the ancient Greek civilization as the student who writes a report about the religion and government of that civilization—which are represented by the buildings of that Acropolis. The model builder will also practice some important math skills about proportion.

It's sometimes a lot easier to get excited about doing research if the end product is a diorama, a poster or a skit rather than a standard written report. That's not to deny the value of having students do written reports to develop their composition skills. It's just about having a choice.

This is one area where technology might be a big help in the classroom. Mark Powell, a colleague who has done extensive research into the appropriate use of technology in Montessori classrooms, notes that "delivering an engaging talk to an audience with images, video, sound and realia (real objects) is a very different skill than reading a paper in front of a group."[11]

Preparing a Powerpoint or Keynote presentation, with all the special effects that today's students master so effortlessly, could be the secret to opening the door to motivation for some of our students.

Powell notes that using iPad reading applications might be a motivating technique for some beginning readers, who would be intrigued by the variety of choices that are offered.

---

[11] Powell, Mark, "Using Technology to Engage Learners," *Presentation to the Berhampore School* (Wellington, NZ, on June 27, 2011). Written notes to accompany Keynote presentation, 6.

"They can read them like traditional still books; read with animations; listen to and follow along like an audio book; record themselves so peers can listen to them reading; and, with some, you can even create your own illustrations with a paint program!"[12]

Even the writing process could benefit from technology-based techniques. Powell advocates digital story telling, "a multimedia publishing genre pioneered by Joe Lambert at the *Center for Digital Storytelling* in Berkeley, CA,"[13] as a way of motivating and engaging students in writing.

This technique follows the same steps in the writing process that we teach in our classes. However, instead of publishing a story on paper, students—particularly at the upper elementary level—create a multimedia story that weaves together text, photos and sound, using different programs available through either MAC- or PC-based systems.

For children growing up in a world where they are exposed to electronics every day, technology is likely to provide the choices in techniques that inspire intrinsic motivation.

Even without fancy technology, there are ways to use our standard Montessori materials to allow more choice in techniques.

We might catch some *unmotivated* students if they have a choice of which materials to use—stamp game, bead frame or checkerboard to do multiplication problems; external parts, first knowledge question and answer, or body functions to study the frog; a turtle, a snake, or a crocodile to study reptiles; puzzle maps or pin maps to familiarize themselves with the countries of Africa.

In other words, we need to take advantage of the variety of materials Montessori provides for student work.

To go a step further, perhaps a student is just not that interested in any of those neatly boxed shelf materials. Since one of the main purposes of the classified cards is to develop reading fluency and comprehension, a reluctant student could be given the option of making "external parts" cards for something that really fascinates him.

---

[12] Powell, "Using Technology," 5.
[13] Ibid, 9.

We once had a student who could barely read but had a fascination for NASCAR and race cars. So we made some classified cards for him about race cars and drivers. When he was given access to materials that matched his interests, he quickly learned to read.

Upper elementary students are much more capable of producing their own materials than we might think. One year, after studying advanced classification of animals with a teacher-made Chinese box, the students made their own version for plants. They learned a lot more about the system of classification and were more enthusiastic about their work than if we had purchased a plant classification set that was commercially manufactured.

Another year, when we were studying American history, the students made a timeline that wrapped around the walls of the room as the school year progressed, visually and artistically representing a summary of their knowledge at the end of each time period. That timeline was never used in the classroom again, because it belonged to that year's class and was their particular source of motivation.

Team

This is where Pink comes closest to identifying with Kohn's strategy of collaboration, which we will discuss at greater length in a later chapter. The point here is the focus on *choice* in the formation of teams.

Speaking primarily of the business model, of self-selected or boss-designed teams, Pink states, "Ample research has shown that people working in self-organized teams are more satisfied than those working in inherited teams."[14]

The situation is really no different in a school setting. Given the importance of social placements for the elementary aged student, we should ask ourselves whether we are providing them with enough opportunity for choice in determining their working partners.

There may be times, for a variety of reasons, when we assign students to work teams. Some of those reasons might be to make sure there are adequate skill sets available to complete an assignment, to prevent

---

[14]Pink, *Drive*, 108.

exclusive cliques from forming in the class, to foster appreciation of less likeable students with their peers, or to force some students out of their comfort zone into a more challenging context for collaboration.

However, all else being equal, having choice of work partners is likely to foster more intrinsic motivation for our students.

Here again, technology offers our students more options for collaboration. For example, Powell notes that *Google Docs*, a web-based suite of applications equivalent to MS Word or iWork, allows multiple users to edit the same document from different computers.[15]

Even email, listservs, electronic forums, and blogs can be ways for students to communicate in a collaborative project or for teachers to interact with students as they go about their work.

Contact with the electronic world can lure some students into productive teamwork in a way that other forms of collaboration might not offer. It can be a source of intrinsic motivation.

Conclusion

If we give our students real choices in task, time, technique and team, they are more likely to be motivated.

A final word about choice before we move on to the next C: if we give students choices, we must be willing to accept their choices—and the consequences that go with them.

If we don't want to provide a real choice and will only be satisfied if students make the "right" choices, then we are depriving them of the opportunity to learn from the consequences of unfortunate choices. It is futile to continually "rescue" children by trying to protect them from their own poor decisions.

We need to trust the choices our students make to enable all of them to be intrinsically motivated.

---

[15] Powell, "Using Technology," 6.

Chapter 8

Content: Answering the "So What?" Question

Meaningful content or purpose is just as important to motivation as the element of choice. In fact, content defines motivation. It is why we do something, for what purpose and toward what goal.

Once again, this is one of the elements of intrinsic motivation on which there is universal agreement among the experts.

Kohn expresses this in terms of content worth knowing, while Drive talks about purpose, but their intent is the same. There has to be a reason to learn something for a student to be motivated intrinsically.

Kohn, in speaking about the typical school experience, complains, "Right now, a good deal of what students are required to do in school is, to be blunt, not worth doing. The tasks they are assigned involve very little creative thought and very much rote learning. These tasks have no apparent connection to children's lives and interests."[1]

So, we must focus on the relevance of the material we want our students to learn. They are not likely to be interested in studying something that seems unconnected to their real lives outside the classroom. Relevance creates interest—and motivation.

In addition to the disconnect with their real lives, Kohn says traditional education is unsuccessful and less motivating because "learning is decontextualized. We break ideas down into tiny pieces that bear no relation to the whole."[2]

This is a point that resonates forcefully with us as Montessori teachers, since we are encouraged to teach every subject in an integrated

---

[1]Kohn, *Punished,* 216.
[2]Ibid.

way, moving from the big picture to the details. Montessori herself said that the universe is the ultimate context for understanding everything.

Kohn, quoting prominent researchers on motivation, writes, "the goals toward which activities (are) directed must have some meaning for students in order for them to find the challenge of reaching that goal intrinsically motivating."[3]

What this sounds like is very similar to the much simpler and more direct dictum of Montessori education: *follow the child.*

Pink, for his part, talks about *purpose* as one of the three legs of motivation. "Autonomous people working toward mastery perform at very high levels. But those who do so in the service of some greater objective can achieve even more."[4]

This takes us beyond Kohn's focus on relevance for daily living, to a level of meaning and purpose that goes deeper than practical exigencies—a theme that also fits well with Montessori.

"From the moment that human beings first stared into the sky, contemplated their place in the universe, and tried to create something that bettered the world and outlasted their lives," Pink writes, "we have been purpose seekers."[5]

Summing up the conclusions of research studies on motivation and the central point of his whole book, he says, "The science shows that the secret to high performance isn't our biological drive or our reward-and-punishment drive, but our third drive—our deep-seated desire to direct our own lives, to extend and expand our abilities, and to live a life of purpose."[6]

Murray, in describing the element of *interest* or meaning, makes note of this connection to a higher purpose. "One of the ways that Montessori education engages student interest is through linking new knowledge to the larger universe and finding connections that will make material meaningful for students."[7]

---

[3]Kohn, *Punished,*218. Mark Lepper & Melinda Hodell, "Intrinsic Motivation in the Classroom," in *Research on Motivation in Education: Goals and Cognitions,* vol. 3, ed. Carol Ames and Russell Ames (New York: Academic Press, 1989).
[4]Pink, *Drive,* 133.
[5]Ibid, 134.
[6]Ibid, 145.
[7]Murray, "Philosophy Reflects," 27.

Lillard, in a chapter of her book dedicated to *interest*, cites numerous studies to show that this element creates more effective learning. She also links interest to motivation: "Interest appears to organize cognition and influence motivation, so that children can learn the most when able to engage with articles and issues of greater personal interest."[8]

There are other ways to view content as a motivating factor. A portrayal of meaningful content that Montessori proposes—as outlined in Part 1 of this book—is any activity that creates internal growth in the child. She says this experience of personal growth is itself a motivating force.

Finally, modern brain science and educational research studies suggest that content is more motivating when it has an emotional component. Good teachers have known about this instinctively for a long time, but we have only become aware of how important this element is from studies in the past few decades.

So what does all this have to do with teaching? How does this apply to those unmotivated kids in our classes?

Drawing on the nuances of all of the experts above, we need to examine the *content* of our teaching on several levels:

- its relevance to daily life (Kohn)

- its attraction as a means of self-development (Montessori)

- its emotional content (brain research)

- its place in a larger context (Kohn and Montessori)

- its relation to the purpose of life itself (Pink and Montessori)

Each of these levels can create motivation in a student. Although they differ from each other, they all weave a connection between the learner and the content to be studied. If the material to be learned cannot be related to the student on one level or does not lead to intrinsic motivation, we can then appeal to the other levels of relevance.

---

[8]Lillard, *Science*, 122.

Content as Practically Relevant

When we examine our teaching practices, we have to ask ourselves if our lessons make sense or have practical relevance to the children sitting in front of us. This is the equivalent of asking whether we are truly *following the child,* as Montessori tradition demands.

Whenever we give a lesson, we need to begin with our own clear understanding of the purpose or aim of that lesson. It is only this clear understanding that gives it value and makes it worth the time we spend on it. But that's just the starting point.

Next we must ask the question, "So what?" If we don't have an answer to that question that makes sense to the children sitting in front of us and relates to their daily lives, they likely will be less than entranced by our presentation. We will be teaching out of our albums instead of following the children. They need to know why they should care about some new information or skill.

We can learn a lot from Montessori's development of the practical life curriculum at the early childhood level. Children learn to wash a table, pour from one container into another, polish a metal bowl, or tie a bow because these activities prepare them for real life. Young children enjoy these activities so much because it makes them feel competent and confident that they can manage their own lives. The activities are relevant—the content is meaningful.

As we teach at the elementary level we must keep this perspective in mind. It is essential to communicate to our students why they should care about learning something new, what it can teach them about dealing with life in a competent and self-confident way.

When, as a lower elementary teacher, we give a lesson in dynamic subtraction, we should create word problems related to situations that students come across in their daily lives. For example, if you give a cashier two twenty-dollar bills for a $36 charge, how much should you get back in change?

If we offer word problems that relate to everyday situations, our students will be more motivated to learn math. Let them see the purpose of whole numbers, fractions, decimals and percents with questions like,

"How much more will you earn if you get a 3% raise?" or "How do you cut a recipe in half?"

But it's not just Math that has a practical side. In Geometry, the study of angles could be related to the work of a carpenter trying to cut molding that has to match up in more complicated corners of a wall like a bay window. Area work could be related to figuring out how much paint to buy to cover the walls of a living room or how much carpet is needed to cover the floor.

In Language, we learn to read fluently so we can be literate members of a society that gives out information in written form for thousands of daily uses. We learn to write coherently and concisely so that our job applications get us into the door of a good company or so we can share our ideas with others in an effective way.

We learn to spell and punctuate correctly so others can read our written thoughts without stumbling over our words. We learn the parts of speech and how to analyze sentences so our writing will be more sophisticated and interesting to others.

And what about History, Geography, Biology and Physical Science?

The "discovery" of fire by Homo erectus was the first step toward harnessing energy that made possible our ability to light our homes at night; the Romans discovered a way to build arches that is still used in construction of modern buildings and bridges; the first American colonies established the foundations for an agricultural and industrial lifestyle that continues to furnish us with goods we buy at the supermarket and the hardware store today.

The study of rivers helps us understand why so many of our major cities are located where they are today. Straight lines or jagged lines on maps tell us whether national borders are natural or man-made. Geographical characteristics of different places explain why some societies are more advanced and economically successful than others (see Jared Diamond's book, *Guns, Germs and Steel*[9]).

A study of the five classes of vertebrates helps us to better understand our own place in the world. The study of photosynthesis

---

[9]Diamond, Jared, *Guns, Germs and Steel: The Fates of Human Societies* (New York: W.W. Norton & Company, 1997).

helps us appreciate plants for their vital role in our own survival. Studies in human biology help us learn how to live healthier lives.

The study of simple machines in Physics can teach us how to accomplish tasks far beyond our physical strength alone. Chemistry studies can help us sort through the conflicting claims of advertisers about common household products.

We don't ask our students to study all these subjects to become masters of trivia, or potential Jeopardy champions. They should study them because they can be applied to our daily lives, because they are relevant, because they contribute to competence and joy in living.

The more directly related a lesson is to the world they live in, the more personal relevance it has. When students don't see that relevance, when we can't give them an answer to the "so what?" question, they are less likely to be motivated and engaged in the work we ask them to do.

That's one level of meaningful content that might solve the motivation problem for some of our students. There are other levels of meaning that go beyond a simple connection with "real life."

Content as a Means of Personal Development

For Montessori, the whole enterprise of education is directed toward the internal self-development of the child. Anything that contributes to that growth provides its own source of satisfaction and, hence, intrinsic motivation.

In writing about the teaching of math, for example, Montessori was clear that the real purpose of all those materials she developed was not just to find ways to get the right answer to a problem. More fundamentally, they were to help develop the child's *mathematical mind.*

In her book, *Psicoaritmetica,* Montessori called her math materials a "gym for mental gymnastics."[10] In more modern terms, the study of mathematics is less about finding answers to specific problems than developing neural pathways that make a more powerful brain.[11]

---

[10]Montessori, Maria, *Psicoaritmetica* (Milan, Italy: Garzanti, 1971), 1-2.

[11]Duffy, Michael, *Math Works: Montessori Math and the Developing Brain* (Hollidaysburg, PA: Parent Child Press, 2008). Chapter 4.

Whenever we are training prospective Montessori teachers, we acknowledge that there is little apparent application for learning about cubing and cube roots. They won't show up on standardized tests, they aren't used in common situations of daily life, they are unlikely to be used in the future by our students unless they go into a field of study involving higher mathematics. The real beauty of these studies is that they are an elegant exercise of the mind for our students to train their brains to think mathematically.

The same would be true for Geometry and Science. The very title of her recently translated book about geometry, *Psychogeometry*,[12] comes from the Italian word *Psicogeometrica* that she invented. The thrust of her science program is to teach children scientific ways of thinking about the world around them, not just a collection of scientific trivia.

As for Language, the goal is to produce truly literate adults, who can express themselves orally or in written form in clear and concise fashion, who can read with real understanding and appreciation of the beauty of literature, and who understand the structure of their native language. This goal gives a deeper meaning to language study than simply learning how to identify an adjective or dependent clause.

One of the goals of studying any subject, particularly in the cultural curriculum, is not just to learn facts but also to develop higher-level thinking. Bloom's taxonomy, named for Benjamin Bloom, is well known in educational circles as a way of classifying different domains of cognitive, affective and psychomotor learning.

In the cognitive or knowledge-based learning field, Bloom defines six levels that build on one another—knowledge, comprehension, application, analysis, synthesis and evaluation—from pure recall of factual information to value judgments.

The higher the level of thinking involved in an activity, the greater the sense of internal satisfaction is likely to result for the student and, thus, the higher the intrinsic motivation.

We can apply this hierarchy to our follow up expectations for work following lessons. Beyond the real life and personal relevance of the

---

[12]Montessori, Maria, *Psychogeometry* (Amsterdam, The Netherlands: Montessori-Pierson Publishing Company, 2011).

activities we ask students to do, we should look for ways to increase the level of higher order thinking involved.

It's one thing to be able to recall the fact that humans are mammals, and quite another to understand that scientists classify life according to patterns of characteristics, or to appreciate that humans are part of a natural network of life.

Being able to list the causes of the American Revolution is not nearly as engaging as understanding that liberty is necessarily limited in all societies or to appreciate that we sometimes have to give up some of our own freedom to protect the rights of others.

By appealing to a higher level of learning, we can increase the intrinsic motivation of at least some of our students. Perhaps some of them are unmotivated because all we are asking them to do is learn a selection of trivial facts instead of using their brains for higher thinking and for developing themselves internally.

Content as Having an Emotional Component

As we have learned more about how the human brain functions in recent decades, we have come to see how important our emotions are in our intellectual life. Everything that comes into our brains from the outside world passes through the limbic system in the center of our brains before it is sent along to the cerebrum for processing.

The limbic system, a complex set of structures that lies just under the cerebrum, includes the hypothalamus, the hippocampus, and the amygdala. It appears to be primarily responsible for our emotional life, and it is the first place that incoming information goes to sort out a primitive evaluation of important or unimportant, as well as an appropriate response of fight or flight.

"The emotional areas are intertwined via myriad connecting circuits to all parts of the neocortex," writes Daniel Goleman. "This gives the emotional centers immense power to influence the functioning of the rest of the brain—including its centers for thought."[13]

---

[13]Goleman, Daniel, *Emotional Intellignce: Why it can Matter More than IQ* (New York: Bantam Books, 1995).

Robert Sylwester, emeritus professor of education at the University of Oregon, writes, "Far more neural fibers project from our brain's relatively small limbic emotional center into the large logical / rational cortical centers than the reverse, so emotion is a more powerful determinant of our behavior than our brain's logical / rational processes."[14]

The amygdala, in particular, is an almond-shaped collection of neurons within the limbic system, which collects information to determine a fight or flight response even before the information reaches the cortex, or higher regions of the brain. Goleman calls this an "emotional hijacking."[15]

Dr. Jeanette Norden, professor of neuroscience at the Vanderbilt University School of Medicine, explains the role of the limbic system in emotions from an anatomical and biochemical viewpoint in a 36-lecture course published by The Teaching Company.

"The limbic system represents a large number of complexly interconnected nuclei and areas which together allow for learning, memory, emotion, and executive function,"[16] she says.

She notes in her lectures that the limbic system, in contrast to the sensory or motor systems, allows us to be *engaged* with the world, a crucial element in producing motivation for learning.[17]

The implications of this for education are obvious. "We know emotion is very important to the educative process because it drives attention, which drives learning and memory," Sylwester states.[18]

Some of the conclusions he says neuroscientists and educators have reached in recent decades about emotion and learning include:

1) emotions exist in children without being taught and are part of the given situation in the learning process;

---

[14]Sylwester, Robert. *A Celebration of Neurons: An Educator's Guide to the Human Brain* (Alexandria, VA: Association for Supervision and Curriculum Development, 1995), 73.
[15]Goleman, *Emotional Intelligence,* 13.
[16]Norden, Jeanette, *Understanding the Brain* (Chantilly, VA: The Teaching Company, 2007) Course Guidebook, 89.
[17]A point she emphasizes in lectures 21, 22 and 24.
[18]Sylwester, *Celebration,* 72.

2) when students are encouraged to identify their emotions, this contributes to the process of metacognition (knowing themselves and what they know);

3) school activities that provide the most emotional support emphasize social interaction and involve the entire body/ brain;

4) memory is greatly enhanced by activities that have an emotional content;

5) emotionally stressful activities are counterproductive because they reduce the student's ability to learn.[19]

Eric Jensen, author of an ASCD monograph on the impact of brain research on learning, writes, "We remember that which is most emotionally laden...Emotions give us a more activated and chemically stimulated brain, which helps us recall things better. The more intense the amygdala arousal, the stronger the imprint."[20]

He ends his discussion of emotions and learning with a beautiful passage: "Good learning engages feelings. Far from an add-on, emotions *are* a form of learning. Our emotions are the genetically refined result of lifetimes of wisdom. We have learned to love, when and how to care, whom to trust, the joy of discovery, and the fear of failure. This learning is just as critical as any other part of education...Research supports engaging appropriate emotions. They are an integral part of every child's education."[21]

One of our most striking experiences of the importance of emotion occurred in an upper elementary class when we were working on the American Revolution. In rural Georgia, this war simply doesn't have the immediate appeal that it has in a place like Boston.

As we struggled to get our students interested in the subject, we began reading aloud James Collier's *My Brother Sam is Dead*. It is the story of a young boy from Connecticut caught between his love of his

---

[19]Sylwester, *Celebration*, 75-77.

[20]Jensen, Eric. *Teaching with the Brain In Mind* (Alexandria, VA: Association for Supervision and Curriculum Development, 1998), 79.

[21]Ibid, 81.

loyalist father and his hero worship of his older brother, who joined the rebels in fighting the British.

Our students couldn't get enough of the book, begging us to continue reading even when it was time for lunch, and most of them broke into tears at the end of the story. Their emotional bond with the boy in the book created an interest in the American Revolution that our lessons simply couldn't match.

As a result, we wound up using the very rich treasury of historical fiction related to U.S. history. We created lists of good books for them to choose from each month as we moved through the study of each period of our country's history.

It's not as easy to find quality children's literature for other areas of study, but we managed to identify some good historical fiction for our study of early humans and ancient civilizations. We also found good books that contained a selection of creation stories, Earth related stories, and animal and plant-related stories to match other areas of the curriculum.[22]

Good literature injects that critical element of emotion into any area of study, giving an answer to the question of why we should care about the content.

Besides good literature, we teachers can be a source of emotional content as well. Those of us who are successful in getting our students engaged in work are generally excited about learning new things ourselves. That happens if we are in awe of the wonders of the universe's birth and the life cycle of the stars, the impact of fire, agriculture, and writing on human existence, and the tremendous diversity of life forms on our planet.

Our excitement can be contagious for our students, just as a blasé attitude toward any content can dampen their interest.

---

[22]A list of good children's literature, as well as multimedia resources that can spark the imagination of your students, can easily be found on the internet, such as Carol Hurst's website (www.carolhurst.com/profsubjects/reading/guided.html) or the Education Resources Information Center (ERIC) site, which has links to annotated bibliographies of children's literature. For a selection related specifically to our Montessori curriculum, see the appendix of our book, *Children of the Universe.*

Content as Part of a Larger Context

Kohn, complaining about content as de-contextualized in most traditional school settings, adds, "When things are taught in isolation, they are harder to understand and harder to care about."[23]

This should not be a problem in our classrooms. Montessori urged us to "give the child a vision of the whole universe... for all things are part of the universe, and are connected with each other to form one whole unity."[24]

The Montessori curriculum is one, inter-woven piece of fabric that integrates all subject areas into a contextualized whole. The more each subject relates to the whole, the deeper the understanding and the more satisfying the learning.

When we study a piece of information in isolation, it's like trying to figure out the sense of a single piece taken from the box of a 1,000-piece jigsaw puzzle. It makes no sense until it is fitted into the rest of the puzzle.

It's part of our job as teachers to provide the big picture—the outside edge that frames the whole puzzle—so every bit of learning fits into the larger context. And it's part of our job to call attention to connections between different elements of the curriculum, just as we connect one piece to another in a puzzle.

Sometimes students will notice these connections themselves, but frequently we are the ones to call their attention to them. For example, we might point out some of the connections between the evolutionary patterns on the Timeline of Life and the characteristics of organisms on the First Classification charts. Or we may make note of the parallels between the Vital Functions of Animals and the way different groups of humans met their fundamental human needs in Ancient Civilizations.

Whenever we can connect elements of the curriculum from different subject areas, each reinforces the other and students internalize the information more quickly. This is one of the main strategies we have

---

[23]Kohn, *Punished*, 216-18.
[24]Montessori, Maria, *To Educate the Human Potential* (Oxford, England: Clio Press, 1989), 5-6.

at our disposal for "getting through the curriculum. An integrated curriculum saves time and deepens understanding.

All this contributes to providing support for the motivation of our students. Understanding new information in context is much more appealing to a learner than studying some factoid in isolation.

Content as Related to the Meaning of Life Itself

We reach a whole new level of meaning in the domain of Cosmic Education. When we study History or Geography or Biology or the Physical Sciences, its all part of an attempt to understand the universe and our place within it. It's an attempt to answer the related questions: Who am I? Where do I come from? Why am I here?[25]

Those are questions that are exquisitely personal—and at the same time deeply philosophical about the human condition in general. What could be more meaningful to our students than attempting to answer those questions?

This is what Pink was talking about when he said content must have a purpose or meaning. It has to make the learner see himself as part of something much larger than himself.

For students to be motivated at this level, teaching must relate to the search for life's meaning rather than isolated facts. Without a firm grasp of the sweeping, comprehensive, coherent narrative of the universe story, we are teaching facts without meaning.

Montessori, in what amounts to her manifesto on the ultimate source of motivation for student learning, explains her concept of Cosmic Education:

"How can the mind of a growing individual continue to be interested if all our teaching be around one particular subject of limited scope, and is limited to the transmission of such small details of knowledge as he is able to memorize?"

---

[25]Duffy, *Children,* 4-5.

She continues, "If the idea of the universe be presented to a child in the right way, it will do more for him than just arouse his interest, for it will create in him admiration and wonder, a feeling loftier than any interest and more satisfying. The child's mind then will no longer wander but becomes fixed and can work. The knowledge he then acquires is organized and systematic; his intelligence becomes whole and complete because of the vision of the whole that has been presented to him, and his interest spreads to all, for all are linked and have their place in the universe on which his mind is centered. The stars, earth, stones, life of all kinds form a whole in relation with each other, and so close is this relation that we cannot understand a stone without some understanding of the great sun! No matter what we touch, an atom, or a cell, we cannot explain it without knowledge of the wide universe."[26]

What about the outcomes of Cosmic Education? Montessori believed that this type of education had the power to transform children—our students—into new kinds of human beings, conscious of their fundamental unity with all humans, with other life forms, and with the universe itself.

This raised consciousness of our unity with all humans throughout time and space is contained in lessons like the Timeline of Humans and, most specifically, Fundamental Human Needs. Whether we are surveying the types of housing throughout human history in a vertical study or exploring what life was like for ancient Egyptians in a horizontal study, the underlying lesson is that *all* human beings share the same fundamental human needs. The way we meet those needs differs, depending on climate, culture and geography.

Montessori hoped that Cosmic Education would eventually lay the groundwork for world peace. Is that not the most meaningful purpose of education today?

All the studies of life, from the external parts of familiar verte-brates to the Timeline of Life to the evolutionary scope of vital functions of animals, drive home the point that all life forms are related. This new level of consciousness can infuse a deeper

---

[26]Montessori, *To Educate,* 5-6.

appreciation for environmental concerns that are so pressing in modern times—giving *meaningful* purpose to our studies.

If we are conscious of these meaningful contexts and convey their importance to our students, we can hope they will be intrinsically motivated to learn how to work for a better world.

Conclusion

The content we teach must have meaning for our students on some level to have any chance of inspiring intrinsic motivation.

There must be a connection between what we teach and our students' lives—as personally relevant, as a means of development, as something that touches them emotionally, as part of a larger picture, or as a clue to the meaning of life itself.

Different students will respond to different kinds of connections. If one level doesn't work for the whole group, we need to appeal to another level to reach those who haven't yet connected to the content.

We have to answer the "So what?" question, in a way that meets the needs of every student in our class, if we hope to have intrinsically motivated students with a love of learning.

Chapter 9

Collaboration: The Secret of Synergy

The third key to intrinsic motivation that the experts agree on is collaboration.

"One of the most exciting developments in modern education goes by the name of cooperative (or collaborative) learning and has children working in pairs or small groups," writes Kohn. "An impressive collection of studies has shown that participation in well-functioning cooperative groups leads students to feel more positive about themselves, about each other, and about the subject they're studying,"[1]

Montessori classrooms, particularly at the elementary level, have been functioning this way for the better part of a century—making it somewhat less exciting as a "development in modern education." However, the important point Kohn makes is that the positive feelings that result from collaboration are a major factor in intrinsic motivation.

And, for him, it's not just for the elementary child. "Cooperative learning works with kindergartners and graduate students, with students who struggle to understand and students who pick things up instantly; it works for math and science, language skills and social studies, fine arts and foreign languages."[2]

Rather than exploring all the research to explain why it works or exploring different forms of cooperative learning, he states, "My purpose here is mostly just to affirm that anyone thinking about learning and motivation, anyone interested in educational reform, must attend to the relationships among students in the classroom and consider the importance of collaboration."[3]

---

[1]Kohn, *Punished,* 214.
[2]Ibid, 214-215.
[3]Ibid, 215.

Pink doesn't list collaboration as a separate element of intrinsic motivation. However, as we saw in a previous chapter, he makes his own pitch for collaboration in connection with the element of choice—choice of team.

Murray advocates for collaboration under the rubric of *relatedness*, stating, "Montessori education clearly leverages the power of elementary children's social tendencies as a means of fostering motivation." Later, she adds, "Three components of the elementary Montessori classroom facilitate relatedness, which in turn fosters internal motivation: the 3-year cycle in each classroom, freedom to work in small groups, and class meetings."[4]

Lillard devotes a whole chapter of her book to collaboration.

"Children in Montessori classrooms have ample opportunity for learning by imitating models, through peer tutoring, and in collaboration...," she writes in her conclusion. "Research in schools and psychology laboratories has shown that learning occurs in these situations. Furthermore, peer tutoring and collaborative arrangements are superior to traditional whole-class teaching in terms of both the learning and the social climate they support."[5]

She notes that developmental theorists Jean Piaget and Lev Vigotsky both assigned peers a prominent role in the learning process.

"Piaget argued that peers are important because by presenting different ideas, they create a state of disequilibrium in the child. Because mental development occurs when the child has to resolve disequilibrium by changing his or her mind, or 'accommodating,' to incorporate new ideas, peers can be an important engine of development."[6]

Lilliard also points out that some form of social learning is recommended by such diverse groups as the National Association for the Education of Young Children (1990), the Mathematical Sciences Education Board of the National Research Council (1989), the National

---

[4]Murray, "Philosophy Reflects," 31.
[5]Lillard, *Science,* 223.
[6]Ibid, 193.

Council of Teachers of Mathematics (1989), and the California State Department of Education (1992).[7]

Lillard suggests several possible explanations for the superiority of collaborative learning over individual learning, particularly for the elementary aged child: *incorporation*, which involves imitation of modeling by a more expert student; *distributed cognition*, the synergistic effect of sharing ideas; *active learning*, because everyone in the group is required to contribute actively; and *motivation*, because it allows students to pursue their natural need for socialization at this age.[8]

Her last point gets to the heart of a discussion about collaboration and intrinsic motivation. Lillard notes that children are naturally more motivated when they are engaged with each other and come to see learning as an opportunity for social interaction.

"This involvement probably motivates learning, as suggested by the studies showing high levels of student satisfaction with peer learning situations... Collaborative learning might achieve its success in part by allowing children to interact socially during these very social years, and through motivating the learning process by having it take place in the context of that highly desired interaction."[9]

Montessori classrooms offer endless opportunities for collaboration, both because of the multi-age groupings and because of the pedagogical approach. Traditional education is based on each student doing his own work. If two students collaborate on finding the answer to a math problem or filling out a worksheet, this is considered cheating and the students are penalized. This is the accepted protocol in schools using the textbook and workbook approach.

However, when you introduce materials such as those used in Montessori classrooms into the equation, collaboration is not only acceptable, it is customary for two or three students to work together.

The Bank Game, for example, is specifically designed for collaboration on a compound multiplication problem, with one student taking the role of *banker*, another of *teller* and a third of *customer*. As

---

[7]Lillard, *Science*, 193.
[8]Ibid, 220-223.
[9]Ibid, 222.

they proceed with solving the problem, each is a backstop to the work of the others, making sure that each transaction is accurate.

In upper elementary, a group of three or four students can work on the same research project about the Egyptian civilization, dividing the tasks on the card materials that guide their research. One focuses on the impact of geography and climate on the civilization, another finds out about the rulers and form of government, yet another reads about the clothing, food and shelter of the ordinary people, and a fourth becomes the expert on their religion and art. Their final report is a compilation of their shared expertise.

Or if the whole class is studying Egypt at the same time, it can be divided into four groups. Each group will focus on a different aspect of the research and report back to the whole class.

Collaboration can make us uncomfortable, particularly if we were raised on the "no cheating" method that forbade us to look at another student's work. It is natural for us to wonder if each of our students in a group project has learned the essential information.

The research on this question is very reassuring, finding that collaboration is more effective than individual study. Learning through the synergy of the group is not only more powerful for the students, it is more fun.

Therefore it is important to ask ourselves if we are making the best use of collaboration as a stimulant for intrinsic motivation.

Need for Inter-Action with Peers

Anyone who has worked for any period of time in a Montessori classroom understands the central role that relations with peers plays in the level of contentment and interest on the part of our students. To deny students opportunities for interaction with their peers is to deprive them of an essential element of enjoyment, both emotionally and in their academic work.

As Montessori teachers, we generally give a lot of latitude for students to work together during the school day, but there are times when we are tempted to limit this interaction in the name of protecting "serious" work. Some insist that students do their math and language work individually; we think that is a mistake. Independent work should be an exception, to meet the needs of an individual student or the nature of a particular work, rather than a general practice. Math and language benefit from collaborative work as much as the sciences and cultural subjects.

Other teachers, because of a limited tolerance for conversation among students, have regular silent periods throughout the day to make sure students are concentrating on their work. While this might be appropriate in rare circumstances, we believe that making this a regular practice shows a lack of trust in students' ability to be responsible about their work while they talk. It also gives the message that serious work should be done in silence, and that school is a place where collaboration is tolerated rather than encouraged—the opposite of what Montessori and modern experts tell us should be the norm.

If we believe that collaboration is important in this stage of our students' development, we have to do more than give lip service to the idea. We have to make sure that we are offering every reasonable opportunity for students to work together in order to experience this stimulus to motivation.

Encouraging Collaboration

If collaboration is a value, how can we encourage it in our classrooms?

First of all, at the elementary level, our lessons should be given in small groups rather than individually. Presenting a math lesson to an individual student delivers the message that this is work that should be done alone, while small group lessons suggest that it could be done with a friend or two—the message we want to convey.

Doing a dynamic addition problem with the golden beads is more successful when two or three children work together. Children who work together on a compound multiplication problem with the checkerboard monitor each other's accuracy. Solving a cube root problem with two or three students in upper elementary makes it more likely they will wind up with the right answer. In all three cases, it makes the work more fun—more motivating.

In our language program, a period of sustained silent reading might be a real struggle for lower elementary students. Perhaps some who have difficulty maintaining attention during this activity might be more engaged in a book they are sharing with a friend—quietly enough not to disturb those around them doing traditional SSR.

Having a student share a story he has written with a friend or with a small writing group transforms the normally solitary practice of writing into a much more appealing activity. And some students simply aren't interested in writing a story on their own but are totally engaged when they make up a story with a friend.

Having students search for nouns, verbs or adjectives in their reading can be attractive to some of our students. But others might not find any motivation to do the work unless they do it with a friend.

It's in the area of the cultural curriculum that we generally have no trouble encouraging collaboration. There are small group projects on researching ancient civilizations, science experiments that take two or three students to perform, and collaborative projects on building dioramas or scale models for the history or biology curriculum.

There may be reasons to assign work groups from time to time, but we should at least on occasion allow students to choose their own collaborators for projects.

Using Technology for Collaboration

Mark Powell, cited in an earlier chapter, points out that the children we teach today are growing up in a world where there are over 600 million users of Facebook. "If Facebook were a country, it would be the third largest in the world after China and India, and gaining rapidly!"[10]

In such a climate, social networks provide an opportunity for collaboration that simply didn't exist a decade ago. Powell cites Don Tapscott, author of *Grown up Digital*, that one of the characteristics of the Net Generation is that "they are the collaboration and relationship generation."[11]

---

[10] Powell, "Using Technology," 2.
[11] Ibid, 4.

Collaboration skills, Powell notes, are also one of the standards for students promulgated by the International Society for Technology in Education (ISTE).

As noted earlier, students and teachers can collaborate using such basic tools as email, listservs, electronic forums, and blogs. A slightly more sophisticated way of creating a common research paper or other document can be found with the wiki Google Docs (explained in a simple YouTube video at www.youtube.com/watch?v=eRqUE6IHTEA).

Collaboration can extend even outside the classroom. ePals and Kidlink are two websites Powell cites for communicating with students all over the world. The ePal website, www.epal.com, boasts that its global community includes over half a million classrooms in 200 countries. Kidlink (www.kidlink.org) was started in 1990 and has been used by children in more than 175 countries.

Students can even collaborate in a way that contributes to scientific research. One program cited by Powell is the Globe Program (www.globe.gov), in which students take measurements of their environment and contribute to collection of data for U.S. government scientists.

This is just a sampling of ways in which technology can enhance collaboration, which in turn contributes to intrinsic motivation.

Conclusion

Whether we are encouraging collaboration within our classrooms or in a more ambitious outreach to the global community, research shows that this can make a major contribution to the intrinsic motivation of our students. Working with others is simply more engaging for elementary students than working alone.

So, we have covered three of the four C's on our list of elements to encourage intrinsic motivation—choice, content, and collaboration. These are strategies that are likely to be effective for at least some of our unmotivated students.

There's one remaining element that we have yet to examine in detail, that of *challenge*, the subject of the final chapter of our search for practical ways to enhance motivation.

Chapter 10

Challenge: The Goldilocks Principle

The one remaining element of intrinsic motivation that we have yet to examine in detail is that of *challenge*, or what we will explain as the Goldilocks Principle.

Pink, who uses the term *mastery*, defines it as "the desire to get better and better at something that matters."[1] This, he argues, produces engagement rather than compliance—a key factor in intrinsic motivation.

Murray, in citing the work of Seifert on motivation, argues that *competence* is an essential element in the pursuit of goals and the avoidance of negative behaviors that demonstrate a lack of motivation. She talks about that negative side in terms all of us will find descriptive of our unmotivated students—"failure avoidance," "learned helplessness," "work avoidance," and "hostile work avoidance."[2]

Lillard, using the term *mastery* for this element, says that children who are not offered extrinsic rewards "tend to adopt mastery goals, and thus choose challenging tasks…When one's primary goal is to learn, rather than to do well on a test, one is less likely to avoid what one does poorly at and more likely to gravitate toward what is challenging."[3]

Deci, who laid a lot of the groundwork in the study of intrinsic motivation, links *competence* to motivation. "People, impelled by the need to feel competent, might engage in various activities simply to expand their own sense of accomplishment. When you think about it, the curiosity of children—their intrinsic motivation to learn—might, to

---

[1]Pink, *Drive*, 111.
[2]Murray, "Using Techology," 24. Citing T.L. Seifert *Understanding student motivation.* Educational Research, 46, (2004). 137-149.
[3]Lillard, *Science*, 149.

a large extent, be attributed to their need to feel effective or competent in dealing with their world."[4]

What all of these authors and researchers are saying is that success at a challenging task builds the self-confidence necessary to attempt new challenges. This brings us to what we have called the "Goldilocks Principle," setting a challenge that will be just hard enough to be interesting but not too hard so as to bring about failure.

For followers of Piaget, whom we have discussed in previous chapters, this means a task that is different enough from previous experience to require some *accommodation* but not so different that it cannot bring about simultaneous *assimilation.* It has to be just right!

For those who cite the Russian psychologist-educator Lev Vygotsky, it's about finding a just right task in what he called the *zone of proximal development* (ZPD).

"According to Vygotsky, the role of education is to provide children with experiences that are in their ZPDs—activities that challenge children but that can be accomplished with sensitive adult guidance… slightly above their level of independent functioning,"[5] write the authors of a study on Vygotsky.

In other words, an activity needs to be at the Goldilocks level of challenge to be engaging and motivating.

Another important thinker in this area is Mihaly Czikszentmihalyi, a Chicago psychologist cited extensively by Pink in his chapter on mastery. Czikszentmihalyi developed a theory about *flow,* which is his terminology for the experience of meeting a *just right* challenge.

We believe Czikszentmihalyi, who gets a lot of attention from the Association Montessori Internationale (AMI) and from the North American Montessori Teacher Association (NAMTA), has something very important to say to all Montessori teachers.

---

[4]Deci, *Why We Do,* 65.
[5]Berk, Laura and Adam Winsler, *Scaffolding Children's Learning: Vygotsky and Early Childhood Education* (Washington, DC: National Association for the Education of Young Children, Berk and Winsler, 1995), 26.

The Concept of Flow

Czikszentmihalyi addresses the issue of intrinsic motivation, with a discussion of the search for *enjoyment*. In his own version of the Goldilocks principle, he states, "Enjoyment appears at the boundary between boredom and anxiety, when the challenges are just balanced with the person's capacity to act."[6]

This balance is the basis for his whole theory of flow. He gives examples in his book about ice skaters who perform at just the right level of difficulty, surgeons who perform delicate operations that test the limits of their skills, sailors who revel in maneuvering their sailboat in tricky winds, and teachers who are in sync with children.

All these people experience a state of consciousness called *"flow—* the state in which people are so involved in an activity that nothing else seems to matter; the experience itself is so enjoyable that people will do it, even at great cost, for the sheer sake of doing it."[7]

They are engaged in what he calls *autotelic* experiences, or activities that produce their own intrinsic reward.

"The term 'autotelic' derives from two Greek words, *auto* meaning self, and *telos* meaning goal. It refers to a self-contained activity, one that is done not with the expectation of some future benefit, but simply because the doing itself is the reward."[8]

This type of activity is one that he says is an optimal experience, or one that brings about the most pleasure and enjoyment one could imagine. "The key element of an optimal experience is that it is an end in itself. Even if initially undertaken for other reasons, the activity that consumes us becomes intrinsically rewarding."

This resembles Montessori's emphasis of *process* over *product*. Because she stressed internal development over academic achievement, Montessori students are often engaged in work that makes the external outcome less important than the process of creating it.

---

[6]Czikszentmihalyi, Mihaly, *Flow: The Psychology of Optimal Experience* (New York: Harper,1990), 52.
[7]Ibid, 4.
[8]Ibid, 67.

Czikszentmihalyi, in his work, concluded that autotelic work breaks through the difficulties inherent in the process and generates true intrinsic inspiration. In a description of the kind of motivation we seek in our classrooms, he concludes, "Alienation gives way to involvement, enjoyment replaces boredom, helplessness turns into a feeling of control, and psychic energy works to reinforce the sense of self, instead of being lost in the service of external goals."[9]

This account is similar to the way Montessori described the look on children's faces when they completed a challenging work, such as the young child in San Lorenzo who ignored distractions and completed an activity with the cylinder blocks 44 times before she put it down and "looked around with a satisfied air."[10]

Montessori describes this experience as a transformation similar to Czikszentmihalyi's description of flow. "Each time that such a polarisation of attention took place, the child began to be completely transformed, to become calmer, more intelligent, more expansive; it showed extraordinary spiritual qualities, recalling the phenomena of a higher consciousness, such as those of conversion."[11]

In order to achieve that type of experience and its resultant motivation, Czikszentmihalyi notes that certain conditions need to be present.

• Not Too Hard, Not Too Easy

Czikszentmihalyi's first component for enjoyment is that it must involve a challenging activity that requires skills.

"By far the overwhelming proportion of optimal experiences are reported to occur within sequences of activities that are goal-directed and bounded by rules—activities that require the investment of psychic energy, and that could not be done without the appropriate skills...this seems to be universally the case."[12]

---

[9]Czikszentmihalyi, *Flow,* 69.
[10]Montessori, *Spontaneous,* 67-68.
[11]Ibid, 68.
[12]Czikszentmihalyi, *Flow,* 49.

This component, the first in Czikszentmihalyi's list of conditions, is the one most directly related to our Goldilocks principle and the one most central to his theory of flow.

"In all the activities people in our study reported engaging in," he writes, "enjoyment comes at a very specific point: whenever the opportunities for action perceived by the individual are equal to his or her capabilities."[13]

That specific point, the fine line between being too hard and too easy, is the place where flow occurs, where a person experiences true enjoyment. It is the Goldilocks point.

When an activity is too hard, it produces anxiety, frustration and loss of motivation; when an activity is too easy, it produces a lack of interest, boredom and also a loss of motivation. It is only when an activity presents an achievable challenge, right at the Goldilocks point, that true motivation is produced and sustained.

• The Sensations of Flow

Whenever people engage in an activity that produces a state of flow, they experience several exceptional sensations: they lose all awareness of potential distractions around them, they disregard all the anxieties inherent in the challenge of the task at hand, they become so engrossed that they lose a sense of self, and they experience an alteration in their sense of time.

That level of concentration described by Czikszentmihalyi is much like the description Montessori makes of normalization through intense focus on an activity. If a child is not totally focused, she will not achieve the experience of flow or normalization—the activity needs to be "just right" so that it blocks out all distractions.

It also has to be at the Goldilocks level to allow the child to disregard the difficulty of the task before her. If it is too hard, her focus on the activity will be sidetracked by her growing anxiety about being able to complete the work.

---

[13]Czikszentmihalyi, *Flow*, 52.

If the activity is at just the right level of difficulty, she can become truly engaged in the work to the point that she forgets about herself in the process. But Czikszentmihalyi says that "paradoxically the sense of self emerges stronger after the flow experience is over."[14]

Finally, a flow producing activity makes a person lose all sense of time. We can see this in children who become so engaged in a particular work that they don't tire as time passes. They don't notice how long they have been working until they experience something akin to what Montessori calls a "wake up" like the little girl she described above.

If the activity is either too hard or too easy, these sensations do not occur and there is no experience of flow.

• Goals, Control and Feedback

The final components of the flow experience described by Czikszentmihalyi involve tasks that have a clear goal, a sense of control over one's own actions, and some form of feedback.

For Czikszentmihalyi, goals and feedback need to be naturally related to each other. When there are clear goals, the person doing an activity receives an inherent feedback as he performs it. She knows whether things are going well or not—e.g. the skater who performs a difficult triple jump and lands cleanly versus one who falls at the end of the jump.

This component fits with the self-correcting nature of many Montessori materials—they give the student immediate feedback about whether things are going well or not.

Finally, there is the element of control, which Czikszent-mihalyi believes is another characteristic of any flow experience. You can't experience flow vicariously, by carrying out an activity that someone else controls. To be in control yourself, the activity has to be at the Goldilocks level of difficulty; otherwise you find yourself out of control.

---

[14]Czikszentmihalyi, *Flow*, 49.

The Brain Chemistry of Motivation

When students are in flow, when their work is at just the right level of difficulty, something happens in the brain that helps explain why the experience is so motivating. When the challenge is just right, it produces a chemistry in the brain that is different from when it is too easy or too hard.

According to those who have studied the literature on brain research, that elusive element of attention or intrinsic motivation depends on two possible goals of human behavior—to promote survival or to extend pleasurable states.[15]

"Under stress and threat, the dominant chemicals in the brain include cortisol, vasopressin, and endorphins."[16] The first two are critical to a survival response and the latter is associated with pleasure, writes Eric Jensen, whom we met in the section on emotional content.

On the negative side of motivation, Jensen says that stress and threat in the school environment "may be the single greatest contributor to impaired academic learning."[17] The reason for this is that stress leads to the release of *cortisol* in the brain, putting the person in a "fight or flight" mode that reverts back to a reptilian stage of brain development. In effect, the higher portions of the brain are shut down in the name of survival. This is not the state we want our students to be in when they are being asked to produce academically or perform on a test.

"It's the perfect response to the unexpected presence of a saber-toothed tiger. But in school, that kind of response leads to problems," Jensen writes. "Chronically high cortisol levels lead to the death of brain cells in the hippocampus, which is critical to explicit memory formation."[18]

Robert Sylwester, another author who links brain research and learning, states that "high cortisol levels provoked by stress can lead to the despair we feel when we've failed."[19]

---

[15]Jensen, *Teaching*, 42.
[16]Ibid, 44.
[17]Ibid, 52.
[18]Ibid, 53.
[19]Sylwester, *Celebration*, 38.

Stress and threats activate defense mechanisms that are great for survival but are bad for learning, and repeated or sustained stress can actually rewire the brain and create a chronic and devastating condition called *learned helplessness.*

So much for the negative chemistry of motivation. This occurs when a situation is viewed as a threat to survival, one of the initiators of attention. Thus, the first strategy to improve intrinsic motivation is to eliminate the element of threat.

On the positive side, pleasurable experiences such as success at a difficult task (Goldilocks, flow experiences) are associated with their own chemistry, the release of *endorphins* and other compounds. That chemistry is its own source of attention and intrinsic motivation.

"Positive thinking engages the left frontal lobe and usually triggers the release of pleasure chemicals such as dopamine as well as natural opiates, or endorphins,"[20] Jensen writes.

"The brain makes its own rewards. They are called opiates, which are used to regulate stress and pain. These opiates can produce a natural high, similar to morphine, alcohol, nicotine, heroin, and cocaine. ...The pleasure-producing system lets you enjoy a behavior, like affection, sex, entertainment, caring or achievement. You might call it a long-term survival mechanism. It's as if the brain says, 'That was good; let's remember that and do it again!' "[21]

In other words, these are good drugs! Motivation to want to do challenging work comes from the drugs produced by the brain itself when a person experiences the satisfaction of meeting a challenge.

Sylwester, in contrast to the cortisol stimulated by stress, says, "On a more positive molecular note, the endorphins are a class of opiate peptides that act to modulate emotions within our pain-pleasure continuum, reducing intense pain and increasing euphoria."[22]

James Zull focuses on *dopamine,* a neurotransmitter closely related to endorphins, as the chemical secret of motivation in the brain. "The exact function of dopamine remains unclear. It may be a producer of

---

[20]Jensen, *Teaching,* 64.
[21]Ibid, 65.
[22]Sylwester, *Celebration,* 38.

pleasure, or it may draw attention to things that look like pleasure. But it is clear that dopamine is somehow tied importantly into what the brain ends up wanting. Maybe a good way to define dopamine would be to call it the 'wanting' molecule."[23]

Professori Norden attributes the release of these pleasure-producing chemicals to what she calls an "endogenous (natural and internal) reward system" housed in the limbic system of the brain. She notes it is the same system that activates *exogenous* pleasure through the use of mood-altering prescription or illegal drugs.[24]

She cites studies she did with rats as part of her medical training in which nuclei of the limbic system were artificially stimulated with carefully placed electrodes to produce pleasure. She said some of the rats would forgo food, water or sex in favor of pressing a lever to activate the electrode, to the point of exhaustion.[25]

Cortisol, on the one hand, and endorphins or dopamine are chemicals that support very different emotional responses in our brain to an activity such as learning. These chemicals can lead to avoidance of a task or intrinsic motivation to want to learn more.

Putting Goldilocks into Practice

If we want students to be intrinsically motivated, if we want them to get an endorphin rush, we must design our expectations of them to be at just the right level of challenge. They have to be Goldilocks activities!

This is really the art of teaching. Follow up work should be challenging enough to be interesting, but not so hard as to be beyond the abilities of our students. It must be at the *just right* level to motivate our students.

• Individual Assessment

When a particular student in our class does not appear to be motivated, despite our best efforts, we must ask ourselves if we have given her the right amount of challenge.

[23]Zull, James, *The Art of Changing the Brain: Enriching the Practice of Teaching by Exploring the Biology of Learning* (Sterling, VA: Stylus Publishing, 2002), 66.
[24]Norden, *Understanding*, 101 ff.
[25]Ibid, 99.

The way we know how to answer that question is through the classic Montessori assessment tool of *observation*. Before we *do* anything or *say* anything about her apparent lack of interest, we need to spend some time observing to figure out the nature of her disinterest.

If she appears *bored* with her work, she is probably not being challenged at a high enough level; if she appears *frustrated* with the work, she is probably being challenged at too high a level. How to approach her depends on which side of the balance she finds herself.

To berate her for not doing her work when she is frustrated by its difficulty is counter-productive and will only create a discouraged learner. To insist that she do work that is well below her interest and ability level will only produce a hostile and reluctant learner.

This is where our role as scientist becomes so crucial. We need to base our expectations on a careful observation of where each student is on the boredom-flow-frustration spectrum. A slight adjustment in one direction or the other could be the key to unlocking intrinsic motivation.

• The Pace of Lessons

One of the ways we can address the issue of boredom or anxiety is to adjust our pace of lessons.

If a number of our students appear to be bored, it may be that we are not giving them enough lessons to create a challenge. They may not have enough choices and have the impression that they are "finished their work" when there is still so much more they could do.

A good rule of thumb might be for every child in the class to have an average of two lessons per day—about what would be required for her to get a lesson in each subject area at least once a week. If we present a child only one lesson a day or no lessons on some days, that might be the cause of her boredom.

Each student should receive lessons each week in Math, Geometry, Grammar, Writing, Reading, History, Geography, Biology and Physical Science. Furthermore, there are potentially three or more levels to teach in each subject area. One way to make this more manageable would be to give whole class lessons in some of the cultural curriculum, particularly the big, impressionistic lessons.

However we plan the delivery of our curriculum, we need to make sure each student in the class is getting a sufficient number of lessons each week to have a variety of choices to avoid being bored.

On the other hand, if a number of children appear overwhelmed and anxious about completing the work expected of them, it may be that the pace of lessons is too intense. This could be either because of the number of lessons they are receiving or the amount of information or new concepts we try to cram into a single lesson.

It is sometimes tempting to combine several presentations into one lesson, so we can better "cover" the full scope of the curriculum. But it does no good for us to move forward aggressively with our lesson plans if we are leaving children behind. This only makes them feel frustrated that they can't keep up.

This is just another illustration of the importance of observation, to determine whether we are going too fast or too slow for our students—or if we have hit the Goldilocks, just-right pace of lessons.

• **Paying Attention to Joy**

When joy breaks out on the face of one of our students, we know she is intrinsically motivated.

She may smile broadly, emit a low whoop of "Yes!" and extend her hands skyward in a gesture of triumph. This is what makes our life as a teacher so rewarding—and what "motivates" our students to want to learn more.

It can be about completing a long division problem with a 3-digit divisor with the test tube division materials; or finding the cube root of a number in the millions with the hierarchical trinomial cube. It can be about figuring out the formula for the area of a decagon with the metal equivalency insets; or seeing the relationship between circumference and diameter (pi) for the first time.

It can be about completing the matrix layout of the vital functions of animals; or mastering the placement of favorite animals on the classification charts. It can be about discovering where fireworks were first invented; or what wonderful things happened to humans with the discovery of fire as a tool.

It can be about understanding for the first time how the tilt of the Earth causes the four seasons; or recognizing the importance of major rivers in the development of human history.

All of these experiences can release those endorphins that create inner, brain-centered motivation for further work and study.

When we notice such a reaction from our students, we know a certain activity has produced the kind of motivation we are seeking. Every time a student has such a moment, we reinforce their love of learning.

Those are the activities that we need to encourage in our class—not the ones that produce frustration or boredom. Repeat joy!

Conclusion

As we have seen from the last four chapters, we can affect the motivation of our students by paying particular attention to the elements of choice, content, collaboration, and challenge.

If we examine our classrooms practices to make sure we are making the best possible use of those four elements, perhaps we can reach some of those unmotivated students who trouble us so much.

Even with all these tools, there may be a child we simply haven't reached yet. We need to keep trying. We have to go back to our toolbox of strategies, both those we learned about from Montessori and those that modern research and science have identified for us.

There has to be something that will instill in a child an intrinsically motivated love of learning. That love of learning is, after all, her default setting. It is what human beings do from birth, just because they are impelled to do so by nature.

If a child is no longer intrinsically motivated, something terrible has happened in the course of her development. We probably have no way to know what factors erased that natural curiosity, and that's not really our concern anyway.

It's our job to create an environment, with every tool at our disposal, in which she can re-discover her love of learning.

Epilogue: Some Final Words

We began this book with the question of what to do with those unmotivated students in our classrooms. Hopefully, the suggestions we offer throughout the book have provided some useful answers to that vexing question.

As Montessori teachers, there should be no doubt in our minds that our goal for our students is that they become intrinsically rather than extrinsically motivated, and that they develop a lifelong love of learning. That's the outcome we all seek. The only issue is how to bring that about.

We are convinced that the majority of our students will be intrinsically motivated if we begin by giving up our need for adult control, and that we support their self-discipline and auto-education. That's what Montessori philosophy dictates we should do. And that was what we tried to highlight in Part 1.

There are specific strategies that this philosophy implies, and we listed some of those in the first chapter of Part 2, talking about ways to support community building as a basis for self-discipline and to encourage autonomy in learning. Unfortunately, this doesn't work for all our students.

In an attempt to reach those who don't respond to classic Montessori strategies, we examined the literature from recent decades of scientific research to identify other tactics that might help our students. This led us to formulate a four-part selection of strategies based on choice, content, collaboration and challenge. We hope an emphasis on these four Cs will reach some of those students who were still not motivated by our competent Montessori practice.

Still, even good Montessori teachers, using all the strategies of Montessori practice and those suggested by the science of motivation, could still fail with individual students in a class. This could be either because of our own inadequacies or, more likely, because there is an underlying emotional issue or learning disability which must be addressed professionally before we can help that child become intrinsically motivated.

The reason for this book is our conviction that the presence of unmotivated students in our classroom will be reduced to a minimum if we do our best to implement the practices of Montessori philosophy and the related suggestions of modern science.

Before we close, there are two issues we would like to address, related to sharing these insights with the parents of our students and with the outside educational community.

Parent Education

We all know how important parent education is to win support for our programs and to make our work with their children succeed in the most effective way possible.

This might involve evenings where we explain the unusual way we teach mathematics—compared to prevailing parental experience and the traditional approaches of society. Or we might make clear the emphasis we place on the social sciences to deliver the Cosmic Education curriculum that Montessori envisioned.

However, we believe that parent education must focus on Montessori philosophy even more than on educational methods. It's important for parents to understand that our goal for their children is self-discipline rather than subservience to adult control; and they should know that we have a system of education that relies on auto-education. Those ideas are more critical for them than knowing how to use the checkerboard!

If parents don't embrace the notion that their children are capable of self-discipline and that this is far superior to simply obeying commands, there could be a disconnect between home and school that leaves their children confused and conflicted. Children don't respond well when they are treated one way at school and another way at home.

Conflicts between parents and teachers also tend to arise when parents believe that rote drills and long hours of homework are the best way for their children to learn. This could indicate they don't appreciate the radical nature of auto-education in a prepared environment of materials-based learning.

Rather than complain about their lack of understanding, we must take responsibility, as a school community, to make parents aware of the long term goals of Montessori education. If we can convince them that the methods we use to attain these worthy objectives are far better for their children's development than the traditional alternatives of authoritarianism and direct instruction, they will join with us instead of resisting us.

In our experience, the only thing that matters to parents in the end is what is good for their child. If we can use the ideas in Part 1 to explain why self-discipline and auto-education are better for their child, parents will join in our efforts and their child will be the beneficiary of this united front.

The Rest of the Educational World

Our emphasis on self-discipline is a different paradigm than the practice in most of our public schools and even the majority of the private schools in the country today. The idea of teachers giving up control to allow children to develop their own internal controls is a fairly radical concept in our society.

The teacher as model and community builder rather than someone exercising class management is an image that is foreign to the way things are done in most traditional schools today, public or private.

The priority of learning over teaching in the dynamics of the educational process, or Montessori's concept of auto-education, is a radical departure from the direct instruction model prevalent in most of the schools in our country.

So, our method of education is a radical reform over traditional methods of education. Our approach is a much more deep-rooted reform of education than simply developing a new system of testing (i.e. No Child Left Behind), or defining curriculum benchmarks (i.e. Common Core Standards).

That means we have something to say in the national conversation about education reform. What's more, the recent science from decades of research tells us that our way produces more intrinsic motivation and love of learning in students than the way the rest of society is going about it.

What an impact this could have on dropout rates, on the depth of learning on the part of students, on creativity and problem-solving, on so many other measures of success beyond standardized test scores for math and language.

The outside world is beginning to take notice of some of the outstanding graduates of Montessori education. An article in *Forbes* magazine last year was entitled, "Is Montessori the origin of Google and Amazon?"[1] An earlier article in the *Wall Street Journal* raised the possibility of a "Montessori Mafia,"[2] given that our educational approach has spawned a creative elite, including Google's founders Larry Page and Sergei Brin, Amazon's Jeff Bezos, videogame pioneer Will Wright, Wikipedia founder Jimmy Wales, cook Julia Child and rapper Sean "P.Diddy" Combs.

Clark Montessori High School, in Cincinnati, was one of the three finalists in the national race to attract President Barack Obama as the commencement speaker at graduation ceremonies in 2011. They had to settle for U.S. Education Secretary Arne Duncan.

Popular authors like Alfie Kohn have written books that not only support basic principles of Montessori, as noted earlier in this book, but even describe our Montessori approach in minute detail without actually citing Montessori. See *The Schools Our Children Deserve.*"[3]

---

[1]Denning, Steve,"Is Montessori the origin of Google and Amazon?" *Forbes* (August, 2, 2011).

[2]Sims, Peter, "The Montessori Mafia," *The Wall Street Journal* (April 5, 2011).

[3]Kohn, Alfie, *The Schools Our Children Deserve: Moving Beyond Traditional Classrooms and "Tougher Standards"* (Boston: Houghton Mifflin, 1999).

However, if we want to be part of the national dialogue about educational reform, we have to document some of our successes with scientific research so we are not just depending on anecdotal evidence and our own convictions.

We hope this book is a stimulus to some of that research and to an identification of the radically different kind of successes that need to be measured in a Montessori context—self-discipline, auto-education, and intrinsic motivation.

Acknowledgements

This book would not have been possible without the support and advice of many of our colleagues. We would like to acknowledge the shared insights gained from years of working with the dedicated faculty of METTC (formerly at CMTE/NY). In particular, Mark Powell, a colleague from those CMTE/NY days, shared with us his views on the use of technology in the classroom.

Several people were central to the editing process of producing a final manuscript. Aline Wolf, a well-known Montessori author herself and founder of Parent Child Press, took the time and considerable effort to make the final text read more fluidly and simply. Mignon Duffy, a university professor, Montessori child and parent, and our daughter, was helpful in narrowing the focus and organizing the content of the book. And Gail Shannon, a former Montessori teacher and good friend, gave the text a final check from her viewpoint as an English teacher.

We are extremely grateful to Laini Szostkowski, a former Montessori student, current Montessori teacher and talented young artist, whose creativity is on display in the illustrations in this book. She managed to capture some very abstract ideas in concrete images.

Parent Child Press manager Holly Weetman skillfully transformed our manuscript into an attractive format, taking care of all the pre-press details, and ushering this book to the printer.

Our dependence on experts like Alfie Kohn, Daniel Pink, and Mihaly Czikszentmihalyi for the sections on the factors of motivation is acknowledged in the footnotes and bibliography, along with a complete list of other authors.

References

Berk, Laura and Adam Winsler . *Scaffolding Children's Learning: Vygotsky and Early Childhood Education.* Washington, DC: National Association for the Education of Young Children, 1995.

Bonnstetter, Ronald. "A Constructivist Approach to Science Teacher Preparation," nerds.unl.edu/pages/preser/sec/articles/construct.html.

Coles, Robert. *The Moral Intelligence of Children.* New York: Random House, 1997.

Curwin, Richard L., Allen N. Mendler and Brian D. Mendler. *Discipline with Dignity.* Alexandria, VA: ASCD, 2008.

Czikszentmihalyi, Mihaly. *Flow: The Psychology of Optimal Experience.* New York: Harper, 1990.

Deci, Edward. *Why We Do What We Do.* New York, NY: Penguin Books, 1995.

DeVries, Rheta and Lawrence Kohlberg. *Constructivist Early Education: Overview and Comparison with Other Programs.* Washington, DC: National Association for the Education of Young Children, 1990.

Dreikurs, Rudolf. *Children the Challenge.* New York: Hawthorn Books, 1964.

Duffy, Michael and D'Neil. *Children of the Universe: Cosmic Education in the Montessori Elementary Classroom.* Hollidaysburg, PA: Parent Child Press, 2002.

Duffy, Michael. *Math Works: Montessori Math the Developing Brain.* Hollidaysburg, PA: Parent Child Press, 2008.

Ginsburg, Herbert and Sylvia Opper. *Piaget's Theory of Intellectual Development.* Englewood Cliffs, NJ: Prentice Hall Inc., 1969.

Goleman, Daniel. *Emotional Intellignce: Why it can Matter More than IQ.* New York: Bantam Books, 1995.

Jensen, Eric. *Teaching with the Brain in Mind.* Alexandria, VA: Association for Supervision and Curriculum Development, 1998.

Kohn, Alfie. *Beyond Discipline: From Compliance to Community.* Alexandria, VA: ASCD, 1996, 2006.

Kohn, Afie. *Punished by Rewards: The Trouble with Gold Stars, Incentive Plans, A's, Praise and Other Bribes.* Boston: Houghton Mifflin, 1993.

Lillard, Angeline Stoll. *Montessori: The Science Behind the Genius.* New York: Oxford University Press, 2005.

Montessori, Maria. *The Absorbent Mind.* New York: Dell Publishing, 1984.

Montessori, Maria. *The Montessori Method,* New York: Schocken Books, 1964.

Montessori, Maria. *Spontaneous Activity in Education.* New York: Schocken Books, 1965, 1974.

Montessori, Maria. *The Secret of Childhood.* Notre Dame, IN: Fides Publishers, 1966.

Montessori, Maria. *Education and Peace.* Oxford, England: Clio Press, 1995.

Montessori, Maria. *Psicoaritmetica.* Milan, Italy: Garzanti, 1971.

Montessori, Maria. *Psychogeometry,* Amsterdam, The Netherlands: Montessori-Pierson Publishing Company, 2011.

Montessori, Maria. *To Educate the Human Potential.* Oxford, England: Clio Press, 1989.

Murray, Angela. "Montessori Elementary Philosophy Reflects Current Motivation Theories," *Montessori Life,* Vol. 23, No. 1, Spring 2011.

Nelsen, Jane. *Positive Discipline.* New York: Ballantine Books, 1981.

Norden, Jeanette. *Understanding the Brain,* (Course Guidebook). Chantilly, VA: The Teaching Company, 2007.

Piaget, Jean. *Science of Education and the Psychology of the Child*, New York: Viking, 1969.

Pink, Daniel. *Drive: The Surprising Truth About What Motivates Us*, New York: Riverhead Books, 2009.

Powell, Mark. "Using Technology to Engage Learners" Presentation to the Berhampore School, Wellington, NZ, on June 27, 2011.

Richardson, V. "Constructivist Pedagogy," *Teachers College Record*, Vol. 105, No. 9, 1623-1640, Teachers College: Columbia University, December 2003.

Sears, William and Martha. *The Discipline Book*. Boston: Little, Brown and Co., 1995.

Standing, E.M., *Maria Montessori: Her Life and Work*, New York: New American Library, 1957.

Sylwester, Robert. *A Celebration of Neurons: An Educator's Guide to the Human Brain*. Alexandria, VA: Association for Supervision and Curriculum Development, 1995.

Zull, James. *The Art of Changing the Brain: Enriching the Practice of Teaching by Exploring the Biology of Learning*. Sterling, VA: Stylus Publishing, 2002.

About the Authors

Michael and D'Neil Duffy have been involved in Montessori education for almost 40 years, since their daughter entered a Montessori school at the age of 2 1/2. After retiring from classroom teaching, the Duffys have dedicated themselves in the last decade to Montessori teacher training, school consultations, lectures, and writing books for the Montessori community. This is the second book they have co-authored, after *Children of the Universe: Cosmic Education in the Montessori Elementary Classroom.*

They have trained Montessori elementary teachers in New York, Toronto, Phoenix, Boston, Vancouver and Puerto Rico. The Duffys have also given workshops at national and international Montessori conferences, and their work has been published in Montessori magazines.

D'Neil, who was a teacher in traditional public and private schools before discovering Montessori, is certified at the primary level by the Association Montessori Internationale and at the 6-12 elementary level by the American Montessori Society. She has taught at every level except toddler and was the founder and administrator of the Blackstock Montessori School in Villa Rica, GA for 21 years.

Michael, who had been a journalist by profession, took the 6-12 elementary training to become certified by AMS and joined Blackstock Montessori in 1989, teaching in lower, then upper elementary classes. In addition to the books co-authored with his wife, he has also written *Math Works: Montessori Math and the Developing Brain.*

Both Duffys have masters degrees in education; D'Neil with a specialty in Guidance and Counseling, and Michael with a specialty in Media Education. They retired from Blackstock in 2001 to devote more of their time to teacher training, formerly with the Center for Montessori Teacher Education/New York, and in recent years with the Montessori Elementary Teacher Training Collaborative, which they co-founded and co-direct. They received the Wisdom of the Elders award from MACTE in 2015 and were named Living Legacies by the American Montessori Society in 2017. They divide most of their free time between Boston and Atlanta, where their children live with their four grandchildren.